Tell Them: Exposing My Deepest & Darkest to Help You Live in the Light

Copyright © 2019 by Caroline Klug

All rights reserved. No part of this publication may be reproduced, distributed, or transmitted in any form or by any means, including photocopying, recording, or other electronic or mechanical methods, without the prior written permission of the author, except in the case of brief quotations embodied in critical reviews and certain other noncommercial uses permitted by copyright law. For permission requests, contact the author using the Contact page on www.CarolineKlug.com. Please be sure to include "Permission Request" in the subject line.

All Scriptures are taken from the Holy Bible, New International Version®, NIV®. Copyright © 1973, 1978, 1984, 2011 from Biblica, Inc.® Used with permission.

Cover design by Tim Fitzpatrick
Author and Cover photograph by James Klug

The stories in this book are about real people and real events, but some names have been omitted for the privacy of the individuals involved and the sequence of events described in the book are not necessarily the sequence of when the events actually occurred. Dialogue has been recreated to the author's best recollection, but is not intended to be accurate.

To request Caroline Klug for a speaking event or appearance, please contact the author using the Contact page on www.CarolineKlug.com. Please be sure to include "Event Request" in the subject line.

ISBN: 978-1-7339008-9-8 (eBook)
ISBN: 978-1-7339008-8-1 (paperback)

Printed in the United States of America

"I have come into the world as a light, so that no one who believes in Me should stay in darkness."
John 12:46

This book is dedicated to anyone who believes their truths will hurt them more than their lies. That, my friend, is the greatest lie of them all. May you find the courage to exhume your bones, walk in the light of grace, and extend mercy to those who have had the faith and courage to do the same.

This is also dedicated to my beautiful daughter, Kyra. May you learn from my mistakes and, no matter what, cling fiercely to the God who loves you even more than I do... which is a whole heck of a lot.

~ C.K.

Tell Them

Exposing My Deepest & Darkest
to Help You Live in the Light

Caroline Klug

Table of Contents

1: Books, Bones & Bras 8

2: The How Factor 20

3: Snuffleupagus 28

4: Bakeries & Bennetons....................................40

5: Would You Like Your Receipt? 52

6: Oo Oo Wait 64

7: Hell on Earth 76

8: It's Not All Fetch & Treats 90

9: Your Blinker Isn't for You 98

10: The Ghost of Christmas Past................... 110

11: Arid Places 124

12: Leaving the 99.. 138

13: Serial Killers 150

14: $10,000 162

15: Who Told You That?............................... 174

16: The Years the Locusts Ate 184

17: Are You Talking to Me? 198

18: And Then I Published a Book... 214

19: Aliens Are Real 230

20: The Hail Mary 244

21: Putting My Bra Back on......................... 256

Chapter 1

Books, Bones & Bras

"Tell them."

That's what God said to me. I knew what He meant. I couldn't plead ignorance. And even if I tried, there was nowhere to hide. In honesty, I had already been hiding, and I wanted to *keep* hiding.

When I was in high school, my friends and I used to play sock tag. We'd wait until it got dark, turn off all the lights in the house, and find a place to hide. Whoever was "it" would have a balled-up pair of tube socks. Once they found us, they would throw the ball of socks at us. (I hoped they were clean.) If we got hit, then we were "it." Yeah, I know. Sounds an awful lot like hide and seek, but sock tag seemed a *lot* cooler as a high school student. I always tried to find a closet and get as far back into it as I could.

When God asked me to share my story, I wanted to be in that closet hiding. I would have gladly crawled under a ginormous pile of a teenage boy's dirty socks and underwear if it kept me from having to say everything He wanted me to say.

Caroline Klug

I don't hear God's voice audibly. The most common way He speaks to me is when a word or a sentence is burned into my brain out of nowhere. It's like seeing a neon sign and having the image of that sign still burning in your eyes long after you've looked away from it. Another way I hear from Him is like having coffee with a close friend and listening for several minutes as they share their thoughts and feelings with me. Only, with God, all those thoughts and feelings are conveyed in an instant. The details of His words feel like a faint memory, and I am left deeply impacted by the *spirit* of the conversation.

For example, say you're listening to a close friend tell you how busy you are, and how you never leave a moment for yourself to rest. She rattles off things about your schedule, your kids' schedules, and your commitments outside of work and home. She expresses concerns about your health and recommends a plan for prioritizing and streamlining so you can have a healthier work-life balance. Although you can *feel* all her words, the only thing you hear is, "You need to prioritize your time better." That's how God spoke to me. He was saying it was time to stop hiding.

"Tell them."

I spent the next forty-eight hours living in a constant state of anxiety. The kind of anxiety that puts so much physical pressure on your chest that it makes your throat feel like it's slowly closing on you. Maybe it would, and then I would die. I kind of felt like I wanted to.

I tried to pray through the anxiety. Have you ever tried to sleep while your teenager is having a sleepover? It was kind of like that. I could feel the presence of God's comfort,

Tell Them

and the truth of His words whispering so sweetly to my heart why this was the best thing to do. But at the same time, Fear, Shame, and Embarrassment were all in the next room, yelling and watching a Transformer movie.

Despite the noise in my head, I believed Him. But that didn't make it easy. In all my self-flattering brilliance, I considered turning this into a work of fiction, but deep down I knew that would just be another form of hiding. I let His request sink in a bit more, and then started justifying why He didn't mean *right now*. I mean, I had just published my first novel, *Stolen*, and was rolling up my sleeves and starting work on my second novel, which would be a spectacular psychological thriller. So, surely, He didn't mean *now*. Because the world needed a spectacular psychological thriller more than they needed the confessions of my deepest and darkest secrets.

Maybe after a few more books. Yes. After two or three more. I took a deep breath, pushed it out of my mind, and tried to relax a little.

"I want you to tell them."

I've never breathed into a paper bag before, but I found myself rummaging through a kitchen drawer looking for the few I knew I had. Did you know if you blow hard enough, the bag breaks?

God was being for real. For real, for real. He really wanted me to roll back the gravestone and expose every dark and decrepit skeleton I worked so hard to bury *so* deeply. Those CrossFit crazies have nothing on the show of strength I exhibited while digging. Some of these bones I had buried so deeply and so profoundly, even *I* thought they were someone else's story.

Nausea. That's all I felt. It's what I feel right now. There aren't enough jokes in the world to make these bones look pretty.

Before we talk about *what* I have to share, let's talk about *why*.

It's about control.

But not the kind of control you might think. It wasn't about me controlling anything. It was about my giving up control to someone who didn't and would never have my best interest in mind. For every bone I buried, I gave Satan an exponentially large playing field to control me and hold me captive through his lies. The bigger the pile, the more fear he drove into my heart. We know Satan is a serial killer (John 10:10), and we know his primary agenda is to rip us as far from God's arms as he can, and ultimately cause us an eternity of separation and misery. Little by little, he uses fear and manipulation to guide our justifications and rationalizations until he has us believing we are better off leaving those bones right where they are. It makes my left eye twitch to compliment him, but he's really good at what he does.

I write a lot about letting go and letting God. It's easy to say when I'm talking about the promises of God or not punching someone in the face when they cut in front of me. Applying this practice to the shameful or embarrassing things of our past is next level. It's especially hard to do when you've got a death grip on anything you think might hurt you. Rather than put them on display, you take those bones and you dig. Man, do you dig. You bury them until you can't hear them screaming anymore. And you make sure no one else can either.

There are many things I plan on talking about in this book that cause me shame, because I was the one who made a hideous decision to land myself in the middle of that mud puddle. But there are other things I'll share which had nothing to do with my bad decisions, and everything to do with the bad decisions of another. Sometimes, things that cause us shame happen *to* us and not *because* of us. But they both have voices. They both drive fear that people will look at you differently or think less of you as a human being. I know part of this journey is to stop those voices. Take their power away. So, I'm about to take my proverbial bra off and let it all hang out.

Whoa. Can I say that? I guess I just did.

As soon as I wrote that comment about the bra, the image on the book cover flooded into my mind. At first, I laughed. Then, I worried. Could I do that? Could I, as a Christian woman and Christian author put a picture of a bra on the front cover of a book? Why not? Of course, it would need to be a *new* bra. Maybe one from Victoria's Secret.

Did I mention humor is my way of deflecting discomfort? Extreme discomfort. So, if I have offended anyone by using my bra as an analogy, I deeply apologize. But I believe God gave me that image. He knows these things are difficult, and sometimes a little levity can go a long way. I also believe there's a deeper meaning to that image outside of something humorous.

Caroline Klug

Ladies, if you happen to not be wearing a bra and someone stops by the house unexpectedly, what's your reaction? After first doing quantum mathematics to figure out if you have time to throw something on to hide lack of said delicates, and determine how many seconds you have to react before door knocker leaves, you realize quantum mathematics is really, really hard, and you just used up all the time you could have spent throwing something on. Instead, you cross your arms tightly in front of your chest, answer the door, and hope it's no one you know.

Hey neighbor. Nothing weird to see here. Just crossing my arms in a tight, angry stance, not wanting you to notice I don't have a bra on, and hoping to send a subtle message that I want you to go away.

If you're lucky enough to be super confident and you just don't care, then I'd like to be your friend and learn from you. But if you're like me, then I'm guessing it's at least a little bit embarrassing.

And don't we want to hide what's embarrassing?

It's simply part of human nature. Satan knows that. That's why he's always trying to use the things that cause us shame to keep us down. The more hidden we are, the less useful we are for the Kingdom of God.

I published my first novel, *Stolen*, in May of 2019. It's a fiction thriller and allegory about sin and redemption. Heaps of sin. Like, prostitutes, heroin, and serial killer kinds of sin. I then followed that up with a seven-session study companion that pulled apart the allegory and offered discussion questions. In writing that, God used my own words to move my heart on the importance of being transparent. Ironic.

If you haven't read *Stolen* yet, I won't give away any spoilers. I'll just say there's a lot of shameful hiding that goes on in that book and, in the end, there's a character who experiences redemption and freedom. It wasn't until after the book was published that God showed me I needed to be that character.

I was forgiven, but I wasn't free.

I needed to be able to stand in front of the masses and proclaim without shame what I had done, both because I wasn't that person anymore, and there are people out there who need help. Help they might only accept from someone who understands what they're going through. I had written an entire book on taking control back from the enemy and living in the light of truth. It was time to practice what I preached. I was afraid of the mess my transparency might cause, but I was causing an even bigger mess by keeping it where it was.

When my daughter Kyra was small, there was one time she produced the most baseball-like poop I have ever seen come out of a human being that tiny. It was perfectly round and bigger than the opening of the toilet canal it had to flush through. I was beside myself. I knew I had to do something before it would flush, but I was at a loss of what I could do that didn't involve making any type of contact with it. I tried the passive approach first. I let it sit there. For hours. I was hoping the water would soften it enough to naturally break up when the toilet was flushed. *No dice.* All it did was suck itself over the hole and cause the fecal speckled water to rise alarmingly close to the top of the bowl. (There was a lot of panicking at this point.) Then, I tried using the plunger on it, thinking I could break it up. This only jammed the poop ball into the canal like a blocked artery. *Oh, God. Now what?*

After throwing my plunger away, I paced back and forth through the living room and kitchen trying to figure out what I could use to open it back up. Let me tell you something. Breaking up your kid's poop with a food skewer so it flushes without getting clogged makes you realize something profound about your life. Sometimes you've got to do something that feels really nasty in order to prevent the whole system from failing and making a bigger mess.

I was there. I didn't want my toilet to explode, so I was ready to deal with the poop ball. Then the enemy started talking again, whispering his lies. I felt sick to my stomach and, within the course of a day, had convinced myself it was enough that I had repented and wasn't that person anymore. It was enough I had dealt with God on those things. It was enough that my husband knew these things about my past. Then God asked me a burning question. One that made my heart smolder in the embers of conviction.

"What about the others?"

Rewind about six weeks. My husband, Jim, and I were at a special worship night our church offers once per month. Those nights are a combination of singing praise and worship songs and praying. I'm not one to get overly dramatic when I pray, but that evening, I found myself on my knees on the ground next to my chair. Normally, I'd be distracted by thoughts of not touching the floor with my face, because who knows what's on the bottom of people's shoes. But that night, I was oblivious to any remnants of dog poop from Joe Blow's shoes. Instead, I poured my heart out to God over my desire to write books that really matter. I was proud of what I had written so far, but knew there was more inside me. Something much deeper. I asked Him to allow me to write from a place so raw and so visceral, that the words He gave me could change the hearts and lives of others. I prayed they would be healing balm to hurting hearts and encouragement in the face of their dismay. I prayed they would electrify hearts for God and inspire transformational change. There were *so many others* I wanted to help with my own story.

But perhaps only the parts of my story I *wanted* to tell.

"You hypocrite, first take the plank out of your own eye, and then you will see clearly to remove the speck from your brother's eye." Matthew 7:5

Fast forward back to present day. As I prayed through the anxiety, I thought of the Scripture above. I know it refers to sin, but it struck me in another way. How could I help lead others to freedom if I haven't wholly and completely accepted it for myself? How could I ask others to live in the light if I only had half my body in it? If God was going to use me completely, I had to give Him everything. Not just parts of my story. *All* of my story.

Amidst my anxiety, God spoke softly to my heart. He wasn't saying no to my request to write life-changing books. In fact, He was saying yes. But that yes required something of me. It required me to allow God to walk me into the light first, so I could help others do the same. I had to step out into the light, with all my scars and deformities and burn marks. I tried to wrap my head around that, but all I could see were Shame and Guilt waiting for me at the stage entrance while Fear encircled and taunted me. Doubt told me I couldn't do it, and I almost turned back.

Then something beautiful happened.

I heard Hope calling my name, and saw Love hold the curtain open for me. Grace had pushed Shame and Guilt aside and was waiting to escort me onto the stage. Before I went out there, Peace explained how important it was to tell my story, and Mercy assured me everything would be okay. I took a deep breath and began walking forward.

Then something even *more* beautiful happened.

It wasn't just Grace who escorted me. It was my Jesus, too. He smiled, took my hand, and walked out there with me, side-by-side. I put my head down as I stepped into the light. It was very bright. Forgiveness pressed under my chin and gently lifted my head back up.

To you... *you* are my audience and this book is my stage. But this isn't just for me. It's for you. Remember that prayer asking for God to allow me to write things that can change someone's life? My prayer is that by the end of this book, not only am *I* walking in freedom, but *you* have a path there as well, if you need it. If you choose it.

No lie can overcome the truth, but the truth can overcome any lie.

There's something important I feel compelled to say. It has to do with Christianity in general. As you might assume from what you've gleaned out of this first chapter, God will be present. Not a mere mention or a byproduct, but as a main character. This might not be your *thing*, and it might be because you've not had a great experience with mixing your dark and twisty secrets with the love of God.

As with everything, there are false representations of Christians out there. There are also simply *immature* Christians who mean well, but get their responsibility for love and judgement a little mixed up. If you've felt subject to this type of judgement, I am so sorry you've had an experience that's anything less than a love story.

> "But God demonstrates His own love for us in this: While we were still sinners, Christ died for us."
> Romans 5:8

This is the real truth. Because God loved us so deeply, even amidst our sinful state, God sent His Son, Jesus, to die for us, and Jesus Himself willingly laid His life down for the joy of someday reuniting with His loves in heaven (Hebrews 12:2). God didn't wait until we had it all together. He took action because we *didn't*. Because we needed a way to Him no matter where we were or what we had done.

Satan will always try to manipulate you into thinking God isn't real, He's far away, He's unloving, or He's unfair. I would be so honored and humbled if you would allow me

Caroline Klug

to tell you *my* story, so you can see He is none of those things. Welcome to my love story.

Chapter 2

The How Factor

Before we get to it, I hope you'll humor me and allow me to include this (short) chapter to talk a little bit about the how. This book is designed to help you walk in the light, so I think it's important to share how God brought me from thoughts to words.

From fear to intentionality.

I'm hoping you picked up this book because you sensed hope for yourself in the title or description. If you're here for the juicy tidbits, then you might want to put the book back on the shelf and walk away before you waste your money. This book isn't going to name specific people. It isn't designed to dig up anyone else's bones but mine, and there are two reasons for that. The first is because God didn't ask me to out a bunch of people who may have done some crappy things to me, nor did He ask me to implicate those to whom *I* have done crappy things.

The second reason is because I can't be anyone else's Holy Spirit. The timing and way someone chooses to deal with their past is between them and God. If I took it upon myself to play judge and jury, that would defeat what I hope to be one of the powerful purposes of this book – helping someone else *choose* to walk into the light.

I spent days struggling with how to lay this all out without implicating anyone else. I'll admit, I felt annoyed. I was afraid to even write this book in the first place, but now, on top of that arduous task, I had to overheat the right hemisphere of my brain. I'm not the creative type. I recognize that might sound funny coming from an author of fiction thrillers, but I honestly don't believe writing those makes me skilled in the language of creativity. If it makes me skilled at anything, it's listening to the One who is the Author of creation.

Then it hit me. Why was I trying so hard to figure it out when I had access to the Ultimate Creator? The One who created planets and galaxies and oceans and Baked Ruffles was *right here*. It was a comforting revelation.

When we view the difficult challenge in front of us as something *we* have to conquer, then anxiety and stress can run high. When we view it as something God has already figured out, well, that's something completely different. Rather than keep talking, I started listening. I put aside my skepticism, checked my attitude, prayed, and just listened. As soon as I did that, ideas started collecting. It was like the parting of the red lobes as an entire picture began forming. It's bittersweet when God gives you a way to do what you don't want to do.

I'll never forget walking into my kitchen, mug of cold coffee in hand, headed for one of my favorite inventions of the twentieth century. I was steps away from the magical

Tell Them

box that returns my coffee to the appropriate degree of scalding when I stopped dead in my tracks.

"It's not about you."

There it was. Another coffee conversation with God. The gift of understanding pouring down like rain on a desert floor, and I was that desert. While I sipped my imaginary tall, nonfat, no whip, extra hot mocha from Starbucks, God imparted some very powerful thoughts. He helped me understand it was all about intentionality. Let me give you an example. How many of you have heard – or said – something like this?

"I just wanted you to know Jenny is going through a really tough time right now. I just found out she's pregnant, and she's not sure who the father is. I know how much you care about her, so I thought it would be good to tell you, so you can help me pray for her. You don't need to say anything to her. Just pray for her."

C'mon, ladies. You know what I'm talking about here. This is gossip masquerading as good intentions. I'm sure at some point you've been subject to these types of good intentions. It doesn't feel *good* at all. It just feels like gossip, and it usually makes you stop trusting the one who shared it. Here's another one for you.

"I probably shouldn't say anything, but I was talking to Allie at the grocery store today. When she was pulling her phone out of her purse, a pamphlet from the cosmetic surgery center fell out and onto the floor. When I picked it up, I saw it was for post breast augmentation care. Allie looked really embarrassed, so please don't say anything to her about it. I'm just worried she's having problems with her self-esteem. We should pray for her."

That woman didn't share that news for fake Allie's sake. She shared it because she wanted other people to know what Allie had done. Trying to make it look like it was wrapped in good intentions is just a disingenuous means of outing something someone else may have wanted to keep private. In a best-case scenario, maybe Allie just wanted something for herself. In a worst-case scenario, Allie could have struggled with a horrific disease like cancer that took a breast, and maybe she had that surgery as part of her recovery.

We don't know everyone's story, and we should be careful with how we handle sensitive information, especially when we come by it accidentally and without context.

I wouldn't be any better than these fictional ladies if I chose to write this book from a disingenuous vantage point, seeking either pity or retribution. God connected my heart with *who* I was writing this book for and why. My heart tendered under the raindrops of His wisdom, and I found my fear subsiding. He was right. He always is. It wasn't about me. If it was, then I'd share all the gory details of those who have hurt me and have never seen the light of justice this side of heaven. I would implicate those who were party to my poor decisions and drag them through the mud with me.

Instead, I can take all that mud and make it about how to help *you* walk in the glorious freedom God has already gifted you. I can use it to help people who are caught in the abyss of hurt, lies, or denial, and need a helping hand out from someone who's been there. I know what this scary crevice looks like, and how deep it draws, so I'll do my best to have the right sized ropes and equipment to help you. (Don't worry, I threw away the food skewers.)

A necessary part of helping you is being honest with you. That includes being transparent about some of the dark and twisty feelings that got me into my self-inflicted clusters. Some of those things are going to be downright embarrassing, but I think it's important for you to know where the mind and emotions can lead us if we're not holding those things captive to Christ (2 Corinthians 10:5).

"Do not let any unwholesome talk come out of your mouths, but only what is helpful for building others up according to their needs, that it may benefit those who listen." Ephesians 4:29

As we do this, I've set some guardrails to help me honor God with my words. Unless I have permission, I will not specify any names, and will only specify dates or locations if it can be done with no implication to someone else.

Things will not always be in chronological order. Although the chapters themselves will, for the most part, float together that way, situations within chapters may not.

When talking about things that have happened to me within a relationship, I will not specify if it was a marriage or dating relationship. I can state a fact – like saying I've been divorced twice – but anything I share will only be in the context of having a relationship with someone.

I'm not going to include details that wouldn't benefit you to know. That doesn't mean I'm not going to get personal because, believe me, I am going to get *uncomfortably* personal for some of you. But those details are in there because I believe they might be what someone needs to hear to help them through whatever they have or are going through.

Just so we're aligned, please don't ask who I was referring to when I talked about X, Y, or Z, when it happened, where it happened, or for more details. What I welcome are your questions about how I got to a better place, what I learned about how to avoid going to those bad places, how I can help you, and why Jesus is the answer to every question you have. Those are questions I will talk with you about. All. Day. Long.

With that said, I'm still a big fan of due diligence, so I hired an attorney to read this book. Yes, I paid an attorney to read a book. It would be really great if you told all your friends about it so I could sell enough copies to recoup the expense of that necessary irritation.

In all seriousness though, I looked at it as an investment. Not just to protect myself and my family, but to protect you too. Paying an attorney is one way to ensure this book isn't going to hurt anyone else. I hope to accomplish that mostly through common sense, but I am literally putting my money where my mouth is to make sure I do this right. Intentionality with integrity. In the words of Montell Jordan, "This Is How We Do It."

To wrap up this setting of the stage, take a look at this important verse:

"And we know that in all things God works for the good of those who love Him, who have been called according to His purpose." Romans 8:28

Our stories – all the life experiences which make up who we are – are incomplete if we pick and choose only portions to share. The rich context of our full stories weaves a tapestry of understanding when we allow it all to come together. There might be sections of your life you think don't match, are ugly, or are unsuitable for display, but once combined with all the other threads, can produce something unexpected. Something beautiful. Maybe even something transformative.

The verse above from Romans tells us God can use everything. Even the pieces you think are ugly or unsuitable can be used to stir the minds and hearts of others. There are so many hurting people in the world, and many of them remain in their situations because they don't see a way out.

What if people heard *your* story? What might they think then? What might they do differently?

If there are things I'm afraid or ashamed to talk about, then surely there are others who feel the same. And if I can be brave enough to bring those things into the light, then maybe you can find inspiration in that, and do the same.

Let's begin with a little journey back a few decades, to see where (and why) it all began.

Caroline Klug

Chapter 3
Snuffleupagus

One of the most horrendous times of existence for a human being is middle school. It's an absolute disaster of astronomic proportions as forced social classification meets puberty with a healthy dose of survival of the fittest. It's bad enough to be dealing with the insecurities of changing bodies and voices without also trying to fight your way off the bottom rung of the social ladder. For me, it was more like dangling precariously from it. I think I would have actually been happy to be sitting solidly on the last step. Let's just say diversity wasn't exactly celebrated in 1985.

I grew up with a heart defect called Supraventricular Tachycardia. It was something I was born with, and diagnosed when I was around 1 year old. When you run or exert more energy, the muscles in your body need to gain more nutrients and eliminate waste. In response to this, your heart beats faster to pump more blood through the body. That's why our hearts race when we exercise. When you stop and rest, your heart rate naturally decreases, until it's back to your resting heart rate. With my condition, my heart would speed up, but it didn't always know how to slow back down.

A heartbeat is quite fascinating. Electrical impulses travel down special pathways in your heart, triggering each of the chambers to contract, or, beat. With my heart, there was a loop in the path that acted a lot like the round-a-bout the Griswold family got stuck in on *National Lampoon's European Vacation.* The electrical impulses of my heart would get stuck in that round-a-bout, and I'd need medical intervention to slow it down.

For the better portion of my childhood, it seemed like there was an ambulance at our house about once every couple of months. My parents knew the attending firefighters by name, and they all knew the drill. Cover my face with a cold compress (helps reduce heart rate), and make sure I calm down and relax, despite the stress I felt from the pile of people who never failed to gather in our yard for the show. *C'mon, people. It's a re-run. Nothing new to see. Just another heart episode. Make sure you pick your dog's poop off our lawn before you leave.*

Home was supposed to be the place to get refuge, but it was just another place to get stared at. Another place to be called *different*. Another place besides middle school, that is. I grew up Catholic, and went to a Catholic school from kindergarten through eighth grade. Everyone knew everything about everyone else, and that included all the things you wish they didn't.

This heart condition gave me two distinct disadvantages that made middle school even more of a nightmare than it was organically designed to be. The first was that I could not participate in gym class if there was anything remotely strenuous going on. That meant no running, no climbing

Tell Them

(which, admittedly, turned out to be an advantage given how terrible I was at the ropes), and generally nothing that would increase my heart rate to over one hundred beats per minute. I got very familiar with my gym teachers empathetic nod, which meant it was time for me to separate from the group and go sit on the bleachers and watch what everyone else was doing. We had gym class three times a week. Each class lasted about an hour and, out of those three classes per week, I probably sat out seventy-five percent of class. That meant I had about two hours and fifteen minutes each week where I had to sit on the bleachers and do my best to meld and disappear into them.

Newsflash teachers and doctors, those two hours and fifteen minutes each week of enduring the stares and whispers were harder on my heart than the activity. Besides the obvious reasons, my heart hurt that I couldn't be like the others. I couldn't do the fun things they were doing.

The second distinct disadvantage came in the form of a purse-size box I had to wear with a halter strap. I'm not talking about a stylish Coach purse or a cute, pink satchel. I'm talking about a heavy box with a strap mechanically bolted on, and it was the color of my dog's poop after he ate the caramels he found in my bedroom. It was a heart monitor, designed to record my every heartbeat for several days on end. The worst part about it were the wires that went from the top of the box, under my shirt, and then stuck onto my chest. I was, literally, a walking electrocardiogram. I can still hear my well-intentioned teacher telling everyone in class why I had to wear that heart monitor and how I was *different*. Yes, that's the word she used. She told them how they shouldn't make fun of me for being *different*. Oh, and I was sitting there while she told everyone that. I can still remember staring down at my desk, avoiding eye contact while my face turned red. I'm pretty sure my machine picked up an abnormal reading that afternoon.

Speaking of red, there was the matter of lipstick. When a healthy person's heart races, it's usually because they are exerting energy. Naturally, that person will breathe harder and faster, to provide more oxygen to the blood. When my heart raced, I wasn't exercising, so my respiratory system didn't get the memo to breathe faster. As a common result, my lips would turn a bit blue. It was something that happened a lot, and I was very sensitive to it. So sensitive, that I thought it would be a great idea to make it a daily practice to wear bright red lipstick to cover it up. Because *that* would be less obvious. Again, this was around 1985, long before prepubescents caking their face with make-up was socially expected. Not to mention I was attending a parochial school where all things south of conformity were frowned upon. Regardless, I carried a cheap tube of generic red lipstick around like a security blanket, making sure to slather it on especially thick before gym class. Looking back, I was only heaping on to my label of different.

I didn't *want* to be different. I didn't *ask* to be different.

It certainly didn't feel great when my *difference* was explained to all my peers as if I wasn't even there. Hindsight is always twenty-twenty, and I'm not upset with those teachers today. I know they were only doing what they thought was best at the time. I didn't know of any better way at the time either. But unfortunately, it just further complicated what would become several very socially challenging years for me.

Tell Them

There were a few kids who were always kind and that helped me get through the bad days. They never made fun of me like the other kids, but they also didn't hang with me on the playground. *The dreaded playground.*

Most kids get excited about recess. For me, it was just another portion of the day when I had to pretend not to care that I was being rejected and humiliated. There's a scene in my fiction thriller, *Stolen*, where one of the main characters meets a young girl sitting inside an alcove built into the brick wall of the school yard. That scene was actually born from one of my personal memories. My school had one of those, and it had a vent inside that blew warm air. I used to tuck myself inside of it during the recesses I couldn't talk my way out of, close my eyes and let the warm air blow over me. I found it oddly comforting, and the sound of the air blowing tuned out most of the other sounds of the activities I wasn't invited to join in on. I prayed a lot while I sat in front of that vent. I didn't know what else to do. I wasn't even exactly sure who or where God was, but if there was any chance He could help me with all the emotions I was battling, then I figured it was time well spent.

Unfortunately, I didn't feel a lot of reprieve at the time, but I got really good at pretending nothing was wrong. I got really good at pretending I didn't mind being alone. Me, the person who scored zero introvert points on the Myers-Briggs personality test all three times I took it. I used to fantasize about being the popular girl, and how it might feel to have the other kids fighting over who got to play with me first. Then, one glorious weekend, I thought I just might get my chance.

I let my neighbor's older sister give me one of those box perms. She was in beauty school, and needed someone to practice on. I had long, blonde, stick-straight hair, and would be a perfect candidate. This was a luxury our family could never afford to spend money on, so when the opportunity presented itself, I thought I had won the social lottery.

Guys. This was it.

This would be the epic transformation that would take me from "Carol ugly as a barrel" (the kids at my school were not very creative) to "Caroline so fine." As I sat on the chair in her kitchen, I imagined stardom. She had asked me if I wanted her to cut bangs and layers. Hmm. Supermodel Christie Brinkley had bangs and layers.

Yeah, man, do it up.

I could hardly sit still as she cut my hair and then rolled it around the little pink curlers with the stretchy clips that held it all together. Even when she poured the vat of what I can only suspect was a mixture of sulfur and acid onto those curlers, I rationalized that the respiratory issues and blindness that might result from the fumes would be totally worth it. There was no mirror to stare in as she worked, as we were in the middle of her kitchen, but my imagination was all I needed.

After an excruciating amount of time, she finally finished drying and styling. She had no more gotten the words, "go ahead and..." out of her mouth when I leapt off the chair, and started darting to the bathroom. Then I stopped. If I was going to *be* Christie Brinkley, I had to start *acting* like Christie Brinkley. Cool and collected. I got my 11-year-old swagger on as I finished my trip to the bathroom down the hall, and started daydreaming about walking into school on Monday.

Tell Them

This was going to be *beyond* epic. Classmates would stop what they were doing and their jaws would be agape. Music would play as I strolled in, pretending nothing unusual was happening. I would gently toss my head to the side so my voluptuous curls would swing behind my back, and I would slide into the seat of my one-piece wooden desk with so much finesse, the boys on Dukes of Hazard would be jealous.

I was steps away from the bathroom mirror now. I actually remember closing my eyes as I stepped in front of it, so as not to spoil one second of the surprise. I took a deep breath, and opened them.

[Record skip]

Had I been wise to the world of cuss words, I'm very certain a stream of them would have flown from my mouth like a Boeing 747. I didn't look like Christie Brinkley. I looked like Snuffleupagus on Sesame Street. If you don't know who or what this is, let me describe it as a large puppet animal resembling a wooly mammoth without tusks, whose head-to-toe mop-like hair overpowers any other bodily feature this creature may be fortunate enough to have. Let's just say my new hairstyle added fuel to the fire, and my fifth-grade year continued to be a nightmare I just wanted to wake up from.

Taunting got physical, and kids started coming up to me at recess and kicking me in the butt. They would shout, "Up for the punt!" as they did it. I was horrified, and used every excuse I could muster to stay inside with the nuns. I never said anything about any of it to my parents, but I guess the nuns did. I refused to talk to them about it, mostly because I was embarrassed. One day I came home sobbing after being nailed in the back of the head with an ice chunk, and refused to come out of my room until the next morning. After that happened, my parents decided to take me to a psychiatrist.

I'm a huge fan of good counseling. I would recommend it to anyone, for anything. Getting someone else's perspective and wisdom, especially one trained in the ways of our crazy brains and even crazier emotions, is always a good thing. But back then, to an 11-year-old, all that scenario screamed was, in addition to being different, you're also broken. That's how I felt. Rejected and broken.

I remember more days than not, sitting on my bed, crying out to God to heal me. I'm not talking about teenage alligator tears over the daily drama. I'm talking about beyond-my-years gut wrenching and pain-filled crying. The kind of crying no 11-year-old has any business doing. I begged Him for a *new* heart. Not this broken one inside of me. At the time, I didn't know what it meant to be saved, but I can tell you I believed He was real. I didn't know what that meant for me, and I certainly didn't know this larger than life untouchable entity was, in fact, *touchable*. I wouldn't learn that for decades, but at the time, I saw Him as my only hope for life. Life on Earth, that is.

It's difficult to do justice to what I felt when I was that young, calling out to a God who was still somewhat foreign to me, confused by what I was to Him, all the while reeling from all of life's ice balls being whipped at my head. But I know now that God heard every word I said, saw every tear I cried, and felt every inclination of my small, hurting heart. I know now that when I cried out to Him in faith as an immature 11-year-old, He graciously set His healing in motion. I didn't receive a miraculous healing there on the spot. I had to wait for it. Not because God is thoughtless or cruel, but because He is sovereign and good. Because in all things there is a path to be taken, and I simply wasn't ready to receive what I couldn't yet understand. You see, I was only interested in God healing my physical heart, because I thought that would solve all my problems.

> "If you, then, though you are evil, know how to give good gifts to your children, how much more will your Father in heaven give good gifts to those who ask Him!" Matthew 7:11

Sometimes, we get angry with God when the answers to our prayers aren't delivered like a meal through a fast food drive-thru. Thankfully, God is much wiser. *He knows what that food does to you.* Even though it might have been easy and maybe even satisfying for Him to deliver a blessing quickly by healing my physical heart, He wanted to bless me so much more deeply and completely by healing my emotional heart. *That* would take more time.

I spent the next three years doing my best to make it through. I accepted my place in the social stratosphere and focused my attention on my studies. I was a good student who kept her head down and did the work. I discovered books, which I found transported me away from the things that caused me sadness. I also found my brother's stash of Stephen King books, which opened the door to an entirely new fascination for me. I remember hiding the book *IT* in my bedroom, stealing away whenever I could to read it without my parents finding out. I felt terrified as I turned the pages, but the thrill kept me coming back for more. It would be the start of a life-long love of classic scary movies and thrillers. Satan may have intended for that to take me farther from God, but God turned it into something for His ultimate glory. Isn't it interesting how God uses things in our lives to start molding and shaping us for His work?

Speaking of which, when I wasn't reading, there was something else I found myself indulging in. Something I knew at the time was a little strange, but yet, it felt oddly familiar. The house I grew up in had a huge picture mirror hanging on one of the living room walls. It was maybe four feet high by six feet wide. My brothers used it to pretend they were telling people where the beach was, as they watched themselves flex their muscles while they pointed the way. I used it to pretend too, but in a much different way.

Whenever I was alone in the house, I would stand on the living room coffee table, facing the mirror, and I would pretend I was speaking to a grand audience. I would even pause as their pretend laughter filled the air. (Because I was hilarious, of course.) I would either make up something on twinkies or whatever topic I felt qualified to talk about, or I would repeat whatever was being said on the television behind me. It didn't really matter what I was saying. It only mattered that I was saying something. And someone else was listening, or so I believed.

I had no idea how to put it into words, but I could feel in the deepest parts of me that something... Someone... was calling out to me every time I stood up on that brown, 1970s Formica-topped coffee table. There was a quiet confidence growing in me that I didn't know how to identify. Despite those feelings, I never told anyone what I was doing. Growing up with a heart defect made me believe being different was a bad thing. And that meant *any* kind of different. Just like my blue lips, I hid things about myself I thought others would find strange or off-putting. For me,

Tell Them

telling anyone about the big dreams growing in my soul would just be another means of teasing and rejection, and hiding things was becoming a dangerous mitigation strategy the enemy would springboard off and use against me for years to come.

God knew what He was doing. He also knew I had a very long road in front of me before *I* knew what He was doing. He knew the strongholds I would allow the enemy to have over me, and the bones – the whole skeletons – those strongholds would cause me to bury. He knew it would be decades before I was ready to bring them into the light of day, and receive the kind of healing He knew would be complete and life-breathing. God doesn't do anything halfway. It's not in His perfect and loving nature.

What are you hiding, big or small, that you're afraid of others knowing about you out of fear or shame? What lie do you believe has grown too big to repair?

On the flip side, what unique abilities and beautiful dreams are you hiding because you're afraid others will think they are simply too audacious for *you* to achieve. Rejection from those who know you best can be especially difficult. If any of this is resonating with you, please, keep going with me. We'll cover one more chapter of some important foundation, and then I'll do the hard thing and invite you into the exhumation. My prayer is that it gives you the courage to do the same.

Caroline Klug

Tell Them

Chapter 4
Bakeries & Bennetons

I have always been pretty responsible with money. Well, except for that one year in college when the lady from the credit card company had set up a table in the lobby of my dorm, handing out one-pound bags of M&Ms to anyone who filled out a credit card application. Genius. Outside of that painful facepalm of a life lesson, I typically did a good job of creating a budget and sticking to it. It was something my dad taught me when I was 14, after I got my first job.

He called it the envelope system. This was pre-Microsoft Excel, so it was the Spreadsheet Jurassic Period. For each budget category, he would create an envelope. Whatever the budget for that category, he would put that much cash in it each week or month. When it was gone, it was gone. Brilliant, really. It was simple to understand and, little did he know, my rule-oriented brain would appreciate and cling to it like wet dog hair. Except I took it one step further (I can sense my husband thinking, *of course you did*). I made a special notebook to keep track of all my budget items. I made different versions of it to see what I could have if I spent less in some categories, and then decided if it was worth it. One could say I manually ushered our household from Jurassic to Cretaceous, but I digress.

Even though I didn't technically have to get a job until I was 16, I begged my parents to sign a work release and let me get one early. As the youngest of seven kids, I had a lot of hand-me-downs. Because I went to a Catholic school, I wore a uniform every day, and deciding what to wear to school was thankfully never an issue. My most difficult decision was whether to pull my knee socks up to the required height, which was just below the knee cap, or push them scandalously down to my ankles like the cool kids did, and risk punishment from the nuns. No joke. There was big rebellion going on in that eighth-grade classroom.

I would be making a pretty big leap into the ninth grade that coming fall, moving from a parochial middle school to a public junior high school. As I looked down at my knee-patched jeans and the army green t-shirt from Fleet Farm that was about two sizes too big, I remember wondering how I could flip the script on that *before* I became the afternoon snack in the junior high cafeteria. For reasons we covered in the previous chapters, this was a very real fear of mine. The thought of enduring more years of social banishment was about as appealing as pulling my nose hairs out, one at a time. Have you ever pulled a nose hair? Sweet Jesus.

But first, let me back up and say something important. My dad was a heating and air conditioning guy, and my mom stayed at home with us kids. We didn't have a lot of money growing up, and we certainly didn't dabble in anything remotely fancy but, as a parent today, I look back and see my dad did a pretty bang up job making sure we were never cold or hungry. There were always birthday and

Tell Them

Christmas presents, school supplies, and warm winter jackets. What wasn't always in the budget for the youngest of seven kids was new clothes.

I took off on my banana seat bike at the ripe age of 14 and started riding around the south side of Appleton, WI, thinking about how I could make my own money so I could buy that gloriously cool Ocean Pacific t-shirt and matching checkered shorts. Maybe, just maybe, if I worked hard enough, I could even buy a sweater from Colors of Benetton. *1988 called and they want their coolest retail clothing store back.* I know, I know. High expectations.

I trudged along on my bike with the long, bright yellow seat, sparkly tassels flapping from the ends of the handles, dreaming of button-adorned denim. Suddenly, I slammed my right heel backward onto the pedal, bringing that neon beauty to a screeching halt. I hopped off the seat and straddled the bike as I stared at it. There it was. In all its glory.

Manderfield's Bakery.

Now this wasn't just any bakery. It was *the* bakery. It was the epicenter of all things sweet and delicious. The place every kid wanted to go on Saturday mornings growing up. The wafting scents of fresh baked bread and raised donuts could be smelled from blocks away. Three words. Free donut holes. There it was. Sitting majestically on a corner lot, with windows wrapped generously around each street-facing side. I swore it was glowing. Calling out to me. I hadn't realized how close it was from my house until that day. I walked my bike up to the building, put the kick stand down, and walked to the storefront, where I was about to enter all by myself. I know that doesn't sound like a big deal, because now, 14-year-olds have already had a smart phone

Caroline Klug

for at least four years, and probably know what the inside of the seediest bar in Bangkok looks like, thanks to the Internet. For me, this was unchartered territory. Not only was I crossing the threshold into a business establishment on my own, but I was about to walk up to the owner and ask for a job. Yeah, that's how I rolled. Had I been able to afford one of those cool polo shirts, I for sure would have flipped the collar up on it before I walked in. Pressing the stop button on my Walkman, I grabbed the handle and strode confidently in and up to the front counter. I was in a New York state of mind. *Thanks, Billy.*

To make a longer story shorter, not only did I get that job after some pleading for the parental work release, but I rocked it. I was the youngest employee by at least twenty years, but they treated me well, and I loved working there. I was a hard worker. I figured my age was against me, so I always tried to go the extra mile, including volunteering for the 5:00 a.m. shift. My parents were skeptical, but I drove my little banana seat bike there every other morning. Of course, I always made sure I was there and ready with my apron on by 4:55 a.m. My husband is probably laughing as he reads this. *Some things just don't change, do they, Poo Bear?*

Here's the interesting phenomenon that happened after I got my first real paycheck, which I recall being around $30 (I thought I was filthy rich). You might think I went straight to the mall to buy that O.P. t-shirt. Nope. Something happened after I smiled politely at the bank teller lady, placed my hand on the money, and slid it toward me. I counted it. Three times. Then I slid it into my front pocket *before* I left the bank, as not to tempt anyone outside who might be looking to get rich quick. Because $30. As my mom drove

Tell Them

home, my mind moved away from O.P. and Benetton, and I started wondering how much I could keep if I shopped at the Deb Store instead. Today, I would probably put that into terms like skipping the Rock Revival jeans at The Buckle and going to Target.

I learned something about myself. I had it, but I didn't *have* to spend it. While most of my friends were looking for ways to recklessly shred whatever money fell into their hands, I was trying to figure out how to be a savvy shopper so I could keep more of it for later. Just in case. Because now I had something I could control.

Control.

That simple word ripped open the vortex of a whirlwind that would suck me mercilessly into a black hole, leading to some of my greatest personal downfalls. Growing up, I always felt like I had no control over the things that were happening to me. Making money of my own and having something to make decisions about made me realize there *were* things I could control. And it felt good. What I didn't fully grasp, is that I could use that power for good or evil. As with all intentions, it started out for good.

Things changed a lot for me once I graduated from the parochial school and started ninth grade at James Madison Junior High. It was a public school, and the last grade before entering high school. Remember that banana seat beauty that got me to work at the bakery so I could buy clothes for my transition? Well, that strategy did help me. I don't think the new clothes helped as much as the upgraded self-esteem I got from them. That horrendous perm also found its way to extinction. In addition, several of the students who made my life a living hell went on to the private high school, so I was starting fresh with a mostly new group of people.

There's one important piece of backstory to know before we step into the junior high classroom. Sometime around my last year in the parochial school, something strange happened. My heart issues went into remission. That's a strange word to use for a condition that doesn't *go* into remission, but it's the only way to describe it. The doctors had no explanation for it. One day, the issues I was having just stopped. So that summer before I started at the junior high, I begged my parents to let me try out for the dance team. I mean, literally begged. On my knees, begged. I would have willingly stuck my hand in a bowl of live spiders and then carried one around with me for the day. If you know me, then you know this would be about as likely as Donald Trump and Hillary Clinton enjoying a weekly book club together. But, nonetheless, I begged. I understood how worried they were. After so many years of issues and ambulances and scares, this was a really big step for them. It was also a really big step for me, but I saw it as a way of taking back control.

After much discussion and trepidation, my parents said yes, and I got connected with a group of girls who committed to practicing for try-outs in their backyards over the summer. By that time, I had upgraded my bike to a classic road bike. It was electric blue, with a triangle seat that wobbled a little as I rode, but I was glad to be rid of the banana seat baby bike. By utilizing the discipline I'd built with my bakery job, I made it to every practice and learned all the routines. I even practiced them in my bedroom every night before bed.

Tell Them

I'll never forget walking into the James Madison Junior High gymnasium and seeing the table set up in front of the bleachers, with three pretty girls sitting behind it, with perms that looked like what I had only imagined mine would in the fifth grade. They all had on crisp white and mint green Wildcat dance team uniforms and sparkly pink lip gloss. I was so enamored by how they looked that I walked right into the table where they had the stereo system set up. (This time, I can see Jim lowering and shaking his head with a knowing smile.)

Thankfully, I was too ignorant to be embarrassed. Instead, I laughed and gave the girls at the table a huge smile. I wish I could say that was strategic, but it was really just the inward reflection of the excitement I could not contain. I found out later that my innocent confidence actually helped to secure my spot on the team. They told me, when you make mistakes – and you *will* make mistakes – it's important to just roll with them and always remember the cardinal rule. SMILE. So, you see, sometimes ignorance *is* bliss.

I think this is an important life lesson for all of us. After all, someone brilliant once said, "Life is 20% what happens to you, and 80% how you react to it." I can't tell you how much I wish I would have grasped the enormity of that lesson when I was that young. It might have saved me a lot of heartache and a lot of mistakes in my later years.

But for now, I was a much happier kid, and my outlook was sunny. There were no more ambulances, I made new friends, joined more groups, danced during football half-time, and enjoyed the smells of Polo and Drakkar cologne that filled the junior high hallways. All was well.

Caroline Klug

In the spring, the Appleton East Theater came to our junior high to put on a presentation of *Kiss Me Kate*. Life as I knew it was about to change.

From the moment the lights in the auditorium went down, to the moment they came back up, I sat at the edge of my seat, wide-eyed and completely captivated. My living room coffee table had nothing over this stage. The costumes. The lights. The microphones. The everything. Not to mention a *real* audience. It was spectacular. *They* were spectacular, and I wanted to be one of them. That quiet confidence that had been building over time in my humble living room was now pounding at the door of my heart, and trying to break out of me like the extraterrestrial monster in Sigourney Weaver's *Alien*.

After returning to classes, my heart raced as I watched the minute hand on the clock tick closer and closer to 3:05 p.m. The final bell rang, and I was off. No stopping at the locker. No chatting in the hallway with friends. No lingering conspicuously behind Kyle so I could smell his cologne. I was on a mission. I went straight to the teacher who introduced the High School Troupe, and I asked her how I could get involved. She said I wouldn't be able to participate in theater until I was at the high school, but asked what it was worth to me, and how badly I wanted to do this.

Very badly, of course. She told me, if I was willing to work hard, there was a possibility I could go to the high school a few times per week to train with their Forensics team.

Huh? I wasn't sure what that was, but I pressed for more. *You say it's kids competing in tournaments doing things like acting and speaking? In front of an audience?*

That sounded like a game changer to me.

Tell Them

On that teacher's referral, I started finding rides to the high school a few times a week to practice with their Forensics team, and immerse myself in this magical world I had never known existed before. At first, some of the older kids just thought I was cute, but when I really started to practice hard and learn pieces, they looked at me differently. The State Competition in Madison, WI, was just around the corner, and one of the favored play-acting teams lost an actress. Once again, diligence paid off. The Forensics coach approached me. She acknowledged I was only in ninth grade, but thought I had a natural flare for speaking, and asked if I would be interested in stepping in and filling the role. She might as well have asked me if I'd like a million dollars and a side of forever curly fries. *Um, let me think. Yes!* She told me I'd have to memorize all the lines and blocking (the actions you take while acting) in only a few days.

Why are you looking at me so inquisitively? The answer is still yes!

I worked my butt off. All I did for the next three days was eat, sleep, and memorize.

We did well that day, and it was a high I will never forget. It was also a turning point in my naive and sheltered life. When I entered the high school as a real, live high school student that next year, that same coach tapped me for announcements. At the beginning of every day, I got to miss the first five minutes of study hall to go to the main office, stand in the little communications room with Principal Ore, and read off the daily announcements and sports victories. I did that all three years of high school. Play acting in Forensics turned into Solo Humorous Acting, which took me to Nationals. I got engaged in theater and did every show they put on, including the lead role in my senior year musical. I was in debate and mock trial. I also auditioned and continued on with the high school dance team, which was always a highlight. And I still had a job. I had traded in my bakery apron for an order pad, and worked as a waitress at the local Pizza Hut. *Four bucks, four bucks, four bucks.* You younger kids can google that one.

I may not have been the most popular girl in school, but I was quickly becoming a brand among my teachers and leaders as someone who would step up and excel.

> "Am I now trying to win the approval of human beings, or of God? Or am I trying to please people? If I were still trying to please people, I would not be a servant of Christ." Galatians 1:10

Despite my heart for Him, and Him being my source of success, I was most certainly *not* a servant of Christ during those high school years. Just like Pavlov's dog, I was quickly realizing I would get a treat whenever the bell rang. That bell was a successful performance, and the treat was self-worth. Can you see the dangerous connection I was building? My performance was commended on a regular basis, and my thirst to hear the bell ringing in my honor became unquenchable. It was no longer the actual victory I was striving for. It was human validation. For me, that translated to acceptance.

Things may have changed socially for me during those years, but my heart was still figuratively broken. Although God was setting the stage (pun intended) for developing the skills I'd need to do His work, that root of rejection was still inside of me like a slow growing disease, and because of all the human validation I was seeking, it was on its way to early stage spiritual cancer.

Caroline Klug

Chapter 5
Would You Like Your Receipt?

Wouldn't it be great if we could get a receipt for every life experience? That way, if they weren't up to snuff, we could simply return them.

"Excuse me, Ma'am but I'd like to return this job that didn't work out." Or maybe, "I'd like to return this boyfriend, and exchange him for the faithful model, please."

If only.

I have often thought about what things I would do differently if I could go back – which things I would return, if even for an in-store credit. But God showed me the futility in that kind of thinking. It was a waste of perfectly good brain power. It doesn't make sense, because we can't go back. We can only go forward. But the question is, how do we do that, when things happen that traumatize our spirit and leave us reeling in disbelief?

This is a difficult one for me, as it is the very first bone I ever really buried, and I want to sincerely apologize in advance to my immediate family and close friends who will be learning this for the first time. Please know my silence had nothing to do with lack of trust for all of you, and everything to do with my own insecurities. Allow me to start with a little background disguised as levity, to break the ice.

I'm not sure what they call it today, but back in 1985 they were calling it "Julie's Story." All of the boys and girls were separated into different rooms to have their separate talks. The nuns and the teachers probably thought they were doing us a favor and making it less awkward by separating us and having individual discussions. They really should have ripped the Band-Aid off and done it all together so we could avoid the next two weeks of integrated recess being about as awkward as a fart in church.

Nevertheless, there we were. A room full of fifth-grade girls and a couple of nuns to facilitate the conversation about changing bodies, the birds, and the bees. Nervous looks and giggles charged the atmosphere and, despite the reprimands from the nuns, kids couldn't help themselves from thumbing forward to get a peek at the diagrams of reproductive systems – which included the male reproductive system.

Holy sweet mother of... is that a penis? Is that what they look like?

I could barely think the word let alone say it out loud. My face was about as red as a monkey's fanny. Let me tell you how the birds and the bees talk went in my house growing up.

Oh, wait. It didn't.

At this point, Al Gore was still six years away from creating the Internet (or claiming to, that is), my older siblings were too busy dealing with their own coming of age crap to want to corrupt mine, and getting any kind of information from my parents on this topic was about as likely as a middle school boy never picking his nose. And if you recall, my friends at the middle school were not exactly in plenty, so I missed out on all the gossip shared on the playground, passed along like contraband from the other kids' older siblings. I came into this classroom conversation completely unprepared for the shocking revelations which would rock my tiny, overly sheltered world.

Despite the brave boldness with which those middle school teachers delivered that day's difficult lesson, the awkwardness still clung to me like a cat trying to avoid water. Claws dug deep and hissing. For reasons unknown to me, it made me uncomfortable, so it was easier to just avoid the topic all together. I felt the violence of Bugs Bunny and Tom & Jerry would do me less harm than knowledge of the reproductive system.

As I got older, I remained pretty innocent. When I was in eighth grade, I went to a party where I was introduced to my first pornographic magazine. I looked at it for all of three seconds, enough for a very unpleasant image of a woman on a toilet with her period to be forever burned into my not yet fully developed brain. I got up and walked out of the room. I tried to make it look like I just needed to use the bathroom, because I was afraid of being teased for not wanting to look at it. All I remember is that I immediately knew in my spirit I was looking at something that wasn't okay, and it made me extremely uncomfortable. At that same party, once the magazines were thankfully stowed back in their secret mother-avoiding location, the focus turned to a rousing game of spin the bottle.

Wait, what? Hot diggity dog!

Despite my aversion to the sexually macabre, I was all about kissing a boy. It seemed innocent enough, and the boy I especially wanted to kiss was *at* this party. Manna from heaven. I sat nervously down in the circle and tried not to look too excited. Then I had a thought. I looked slowly around the circle at the other boys who were sitting there. *Hmm. Not the boys I would want to kiss.* Then I counted them and calculated the odds of me being able to kiss the fan favorite. Not very good odds. Whoever said, "You have to kiss a lot of toads before you get the prince" must have played spin the bottle.

 I wasn't allowed to date until I turned 16 but, once I did, I dated a lot. All of that Polo and Drakkar had seeped its way into my Medulla Oblongata, and the mad boy crush was on. But I never did more than kiss. Reflecting back, I'm guessing that's why I never really dated anyone for that long in high school, which was just fine with me, because there were a *lot* of boys out there to kiss, and *somebody* had to kiss them. In all of it, I was pretty innocent. In fact, another scene in my novel, *Stolen*, was also born out of a personal experience of mine involving a ginger soccer player:

> *"She recalled earlier in the year when she made out with Alex Draper. He was a ginger soccer player and all the girls swooned over him. She felt elated to be making out with him, but when he tried to unbutton her jeans, she bolted to her feet and screamed at him for his inappropriate behavior. She thought he wanted to have sex with her, and she had already made up her mind to wait until marriage. The poor kid was so scared, he ran out the door and all the way home, long soccer hair flapping in the wind behind him."*

 There was a time in high school when I accepted an invitation to a popular dance. The dance was fine, and the

Tell Them

night ended with a smile and a wave. He was nice, but I wasn't that into him. The next week at school, one of my friends who was on the football team relayed a story that at first made me angry, but later made me laugh. Apparently, while the football team got ready for practice that Monday following the dance, they were all talking about their weekend conquests. Someone asked the boy who took me how his date went, and he told them we slept together. As conveyed to me, there was total silence in the locker room, followed by abrupt laughter. That's the reputation I had for keeping my legs closed. No one even believed him.

That innocence carried its way into college. Looking back, I'm extremely grateful how much God protected me early on. I had rushed a sorority and, even though I looked 12, could get into all the popular bars because the bouncers were Greek. There were several evenings I was feeling no pain, and let the guy who was buying me drinks walk me back to my dorm room. Weren't they surprised when we got to the door and I thanked them and wished them a good night? I really wasn't wise to the ways of that world back then, and I'm lucky things didn't go as south as they could have. Until that night.

Sometimes it's not the unknown that hurts you, but the known. I liked him, and I thought he liked me. I felt safe with him because he was much bigger than me, and well built. My roommate was out with us, and she had proclaimed loudly to the entire group she would not be coming home that night, as she draped herself over a tall, dark, and handsome guy whose name she didn't know, and left the bar. I thought it was funny at the time. It was late, so we left too, and he walked me back to my dorm. Once we got to the room, he wanted to mess around. I started to go there, but I didn't want to *keep* going there.

I told him I wasn't ready but he kept pressuring. Intimidation is a fickle thing. It can make people respond much differently than you might think. The funny thing is, I never actually said the word, "no." My innocence and inexperience left me believing I had opened a door I couldn't close. My fear of his forceful intimidation kept me silent, although my body language clearly said what my mouth was having trouble forming. I was unprepared in every way possible – mentally, emotionally, and physically. *But I didn't say no. Why didn't I just say no?*

That night, he took something that didn't belong to him, and I can never fully get that back. But for decades, I never told anyone because I thought it was my fault. I thought because I never actually said the word, no, I couldn't call it what it felt like.

I knew there were things I should have done differently, which caused an unhealthy dose of guilt. But a bigger part of me was ashamed. I felt like I had opened that magazine from my ninth-grade party, only I was a part of the picture. I felt dirty. Used. Broken. I could hardly process what had happened. I sat curled up in the corner on my bed, uncertain what to even do. Every part of me wanted to call my dad, but I was caught between Shame and Fear. Shame told me my dad would be disappointed I had even gotten myself into that situation, and would never see me the same way again. Fear convinced me Dad would pull me out of college and that would be the end of any big dreams.

Whatever Shame says is always rooted in a lie. Satan wanted me to believe that going to my dad would only make things worse. But the truth was, I was close to my dad, and knew how much he loved me and was proud of me. As a parent today, the thought of my own daughter enduring something like that, and then quietly suffering alone makes me outraged. I have to disconnect. I can barely process that thought. I know the truth now. I know I should have picked up that phone and let my dad into my deepest and darkest hurt. He would have loved me through it and helped me through whatever steps were necessary to heal.

Loved One, please see the deeper message I'm talking about – one we too often overlook. Our heavenly Father doesn't shame. He loves. He heals. But He can't do that unless we let Him into our deepest and darkest hurts. God is the real gentleman. He never forces our acceptance of Him. He waits for us to ask Him in. Satan uses Shame and Guilt to make us think we can't approach God. Nothing could be farther from the truth.

"Come to Me, all you who are weary and burdened, and I will give you rest." Matthew 11:28

As far as fear is concerned, I had a big one in terms of my long-term plans. I had been the only one in my family to graduate from college. Neither of my parents went, and there wasn't a lot of knowledge or urgency at the time over the benefit or importance of it. I was thankful for the guidance counselor who asked me my senior year if I was planning on participating in the last opportunity to take the ACTs, so I could apply to colleges.
What are the ACTs?
That's exactly what I said. I still remember her pursing her lips together in what I can only assume was disbelief.

Caroline Klug

After a brief conversation, I registered for the class. I didn't study for it. I didn't know I could. I just showed up with my number two pencil, hunkered down, and did the best I could. Thankfully, my best was enough. But fast forward through exciting acceptance letters, dorm room assignments, and the first disillusioning experience with the campus cafeteria, and here I was, pressed into the corner of my dorm room, afraid to lose it all. That was where I made my biggest mistake. I didn't trust what I knew about my dad and his character. I allowed Fear to control me and send me down a path that would cause more long-term pain than that night ever could on its own.

That boy thanked me before he left. Like I had offered him something and he accepted it. Can I just tell you, those two little words messed with my mind in seismic proportions? It made me feel that I *did* offer him something, like I *did* do or say something that made him think it was okay. *Why else would he say something like that?* I didn't know the answers to these questions, but those two words haunted me for years, and fueled all the bad reasons I never told anyone. It wasn't until I finally said it out loud to a counselor ten years after the fact that those words stopped haunting me. Mostly because of the truth that counselor was able to help me see.

It took me a really long time to even tell Jim about it, because I still get caught up in wondering if it was my fault. I even considered leaving this chapter out of this book. And then I watched a popular series on Netflix, *13 Reasons Why*, to see what the kids were talking about, and because I knew Kyra had watched it. It's about a high school student who commits suicide, and leaves a series of old school cassette tapes behind explaining the thirteen reasons she did it. Each tape points to a different person, and one of them is a boy who raped her. When I watched that scene, I found myself crying. For the first time, it wasn't the knockdown, drag out, screaming scene I had been accustomed to in movies, which made me feel like my encounter wasn't the same thing. It was quiet and frightening. *Like mine*. And she never said the word no either, but it was clear to the audience what he had done. I know there are mixed feelings on that series, and I'm not here to speak to that, but that episode is a big reason I left this chapter in. It has strangely been a part of my own healing process, decades after the fact.

For the longest time, I refused to view what happened to me as trauma. I've had a lot of challenging things thrown my way in life but had always refused to see myself as a victim. And if I was tempted by those emotions, I would overcome them by convincing myself I could take control back – somehow – and not allow those situations to keep me down. One might call this a strength or even a blessing. It can be, but it was harmful because, for me, taking control didn't mean dealing with it. It meant burying it.

The difficult thing about trauma is that it can impact a person in deeper ways than what is obvious on the surface. What I'm about to say took a handful of therapy sessions to hear, and several years to come to terms with. And before I say it, I'd like to throw out the disclaimer that this is going to sound really screwed up... because it is.

Remember that root of rejection? One of the things my counselor helped me see is, beyond all the obvious hurt associated with what happened, there was an element of rejection I experienced. That boy didn't want all of me. He only wanted a small part of me. He used what he wanted and threw the rest away. He threw away what I call the beautiful parts – everything that made up my personality, the person I was, and the person I dreamed of being. He didn't see enough value in me to respect me and, instead, left me hurt and discarded like garbage. That feeling was something I was too embarrassed to admit at the time. But it was true. That awful nightmare only fed my label of *rejected*.

Boy from the dorm room that night – if, by God's hand, you end up with this book in *your* hand, then I want you to know something. I forgive you. You see, it has taken me north of two decades to live enough life, walk through enough valleys, and make enough mistakes to realize that it wasn't me who was unworthy. It was you who was hurting in some way. It was yourself you denied, and I'm so sorry you were hurting so much that you felt what you did was an acceptable way to fill whatever void you felt. I hope you found Jesus and, in doing so, have found peace.

At the time, I found my way through it by burying it deeply. So deeply, that false joy was my mask. Rather than retreat, I lived out in the open and put every acting skill I had into practice to play the role of the carefree college student. I continued to go to parties – though I never again allowed someone to walk me home – I danced at football games, and I went home to see my family and told them all how great college was. I even started dating again. Because that's what normal, unbroken people do. In my mind, that was the only option. There was no returning this one. Besides, you can't get a receipt for something you didn't buy.

I convinced myself control was a tool. It was a coping mechanism and a means to protect me from further trauma.

Tell Them

I capitalized on my self-drive and started focusing it on my career. Thinking ahead has always been both a blessing and a curse for me. On the blessing side, I'm really good at risk mitigation because I intentionally think three steps ahead and try to identify all the possible outcomes, and what I could do to rectify known roadblocks.

For example, as a major in Management Information Systems (MIS), I thought it wise to get involved in the MIS club, which was a professional organization for all MIS majors, designed to facilitate growth in your field and provide networking opportunities with both like-minded individuals and professionals in the field. They host a banquet every spring, attended by all MIS majors, MIS professors, and all the corporate suits from the representing companies looking for new employees. When I attended my first one, it didn't take me long to recognize a golden opportunity. I learned that each spring, whoever was the President of the MIS Club got to be the Master of Ceremonies at the banquet. They also got to deliver a speech at that banquet.

Speaking and presenting was a strong skill of mine. If I could get myself to the podium in front of those corporate storks all carrying full-time employment babies, then I'd be set.

After some research, I learned whoever got elected President-Elect in the fall semester was auto-magically the President in the spring. I knew I couldn't just run for President-Elect without having credibility and backing, so I first ran for and secured the Secretary position, and then went on to Treasurer. Once I got to the semester before I graduated, I threw my carefully planned and prayed-for Hail Mary to secure President-Elect. It happened. That spring, I transitioned to the Presidency, and Master of Ceremonies at the banquet, where I crushed the speech I delivered without notes and with constant eye contact. Two weeks later, and a good three months before graduation, I accepted an offer from the Kimberly-Clark Corporation, the most sought-after employer in the state at the time, to start upon graduation.

For as much of a high as this was, it was also a death spiral. It was more fuel for the fire of my identity and acceptance being rooted in my career and performance. My career start was bright, but my personal life was a hot mess.

Ready to do some more digging?

Chapter 6

Oo Oo Wait

I don't know why or when I developed this funny habit, but Jim was the first person to call me out on it. Whenever I start feeling reluctant or nervous about something, I spit out the words "Oo oo wait" in varying degrees, depending on the seriousness of the situation. For example, if I dribble food on my shirt (which happens on a daily basis), I say, "Oo." If I'm trying to step down into the dinghy and it's moving away from the dock a little, I say, "Oo oo." If Jim comes home feeling good after a CrossFit class, picks me up, and tries to hold me over his head like a barbell, I say, "Oo oo wait." The length of the phrase I use is in direct correlation to how threatened I feel about what's happening to me.

★★★

When I was little, my dad would take my siblings and me to Mary's Restaurant for a turtle sundae. He figured the time it took us to eat them, was his chance to impart his many pearls of wisdom to us. All the experiences and lessons he had gathered during life's journey were neatly bundled and crisply articulated for the benefit of his children. At the time, I don't think I truly realized the value of Dad's words but, nevertheless, was smart enough to tuck them safely into my own drawer of wisdom. As I grew older, turtle sundaes turned into Sunday morning breakfast, backyard lawn chairs and coffee, and walks through the woods. I came to cherish those times, and my appreciation for them grew with each one of his carefully chosen words.

My dad may not have been a rich businessman, doctor, or some other socially upscale man, but he was certainly wise beyond his years and had a gift for sharing that wisdom. He taught me so many things and made me so much of who I am. More times than I can count, he would look hard into my eyes until he was certain I was eagerly paying attention. Then he would say with as much certainty as he could,

"Babes, you can be *anything* you want to be."

I would laugh and say, "Not *anything,* Dad."

He would smile with even more determination than before and say, "Yes, *anything.*" He taught me what it meant to be passionate about life and people. He taught me what it meant to fall in love with the simple things in life. He taught me about God and what it meant to truly love Him and the hope, joy, and peace that came with that. His words were strong and comforting, and most of all, loving. I didn't always connect right away with the things he said about God in a way that I could *feel,* but I tucked the ideas away in a safe spot.

My dad spent a lot of time trying to teach me how to be a good decision maker and the importance of being comfortable making those decisions. I was a pretty good kid and he gave me a lot of freedom. He would always work through my problems with me, but ultimately, he would let me make the final decisions, so I would be invested in them and grow from them.

It was October 23, 1995, and I was sitting at the desk of my part-time college job, entering roll slit dimensions for custom paper roll orders. That's when I got the call from my sister telling me Dad was in a hospital in Michigan after having a heart attack. There was no more information. I tried hard through my tears to collect my head and figure out how I was going to get to him. As I was about to leave, the phone rang again. This time, my sister's voice was a fraction of her once concerned but take-charge tone.

"He's gone. Dad's gone."

I don't remember much of what she said after those words. I put the receiver down, laid my head on the desk, and sobbed. A girl I worked with was kind enough to give me a ride home. Over the next few days, while we waited for his body to be transported back to Wisconsin, I grieved, but not completely. I wanted to believe whoever's body they were transporting back home wasn't Dad's. I wanted to believe we were going to walk into that funeral home and see someone unfamiliar to us. I wanted to believe we were going to get a call from him at any moment, explaining he was on a job site somewhere and didn't even know what was going on. That call never came, and neither did the luxury of seeing an unfamiliar face in the casket.

I felt like I had lost the only person in this whole world who really knew who I was. The only person who really believed I could *be* something special. I grieved for a long time. Then I got angry. The kind of angry that stifles your tears. It places its unhealthy filter on your thoughts and corrupts your outlook. I started questioning everything my dad had ever told me about this loving God. If God was so loving, why would He take the only person I needed? Not just wanted. *Needed.* I was only 21. I was too young to lose someone so vital to me. My world felt shaken, and there was only one person I thought could help me, but his absence was the source of my pain. It was like a cruel and circular maze I couldn't find my way out of.

I'm thankful for my brothers and sisters. I was a mess with a lot to sort out, and didn't completely appreciate how much they were there for me at the time, especially my sister, Suzy, and her husband. They stepped up in ways no child should ever have to when dealing with the death of their dad. We all did, really. By all rules of love and nature, we were abandoned by someone who had no right abandoning us. This was a difficult time when we most needed some kind of stability. It was one of the first deeply disturbing life experiences I had ever had – worse than any ice ball thrown at me in middle school.

I had just lost what I felt was my single source of acceptance. My root of rejection was growing deeper by the day, and I had no suitable remedy. God wasn't an option anymore because, in my mind, He had rejected me too. He couldn't possibly love me if He would knowingly cause me so much hurt. I realize what I'm about to say might sound like a lot of psychobabble, but I think there's a good reason why it's earned its way into a lot of psychology books.

In the absence of a father figure – both my earthly father and the ignorance of my heavenly Father – I began subconsciously searching for a substitute. The next fifteen years of my life could really be summed up with one boisterous "Oo oo wait."

Tell Them

There is a book series by Daniel Handler, under the pen name of Lemony Snicket. It's called *A Series of Unfortunate Events*, which would have been an excellent title for the series of relationships that marred the landscape of my twenties and thirties. I was married and divorced twice, entered into multiple unhealthy relationships that did nothing for me emotionally or spiritually, was cheated on more times than I can count, abandoned by people close to me, and made several really awful life decisions that landed me so far from Happy Town that I needed a Hennessey Venom F5 to get me back before life closed shop for the day.

I'll be going into more detail on this later on, but before I do, I want to say one thing up front.

In all of the badness and sadness that existed over the next few decades, there was one thing I will always call a blessing. Quite literally born out of the ashes of those messes was my beautiful daughter, Kyra.

"The light shines in the darkness, and the darkness has not overcome it." John 1:5

God is so good. Despite the choices we make and the darkness we live in, He is able to use all things for good and shine His light in ways that touch and bless our lives forever. For me, Kyra is one of those blessings. I can't imagine any part of my life without her bright eyes and contagious laughter. What's even better is that God has blessed her with some amazing musical gifts and talents, and I can't wait to see how He uses them, and her, to bless the world. Talk about giving thanks. (I sure do.)

Now that we have that clarified up front, I'd like to hop, skip, and jump around a little so you have an idea of just what a train wreck those decades were. Or rather, *I* was.

First, a confession. Okay, this whole book is a confession, but this is an especially stupid one. I like watching *The Bachelor* and *The Bachelorette*. You know, the television series on ABC where piles of men or women all date the same person for like thirty seconds to see if they can find *the one*. I'm currently watching *The Bachelorette*, which started out with thirty men all dating the same woman. Every week, a few of the poor schlubs are denied the coveted rose, which means they leave the show, and the Bachelorette moves on with the remaining men. Inevitably, they all start to go a little stir crazy as jealousy and testosterone get the best of them. Eventually, she whittles it down to the final two, which ends in a final proposal and lots of jumping up and down. *Were you really surprised he proposed after you asked him four times if he would?*

Don't look at me like that. It's spectacular psychological entertainment. It is the quintessential train wreck you can't look away from because we, the viewers, have all the answers. We can see behind all the cameras, and are privy to the side conversations our Bachelorette will never hear until she's sitting side-by-side with her last man standing, watching the live show. I have often thought how interesting it would be to be a butterfly on the wall (I would never want to be a fly because they eat poop) and watch her facial expressions as she sees her own train cars pile on top of each other. Would she see or hear something that would have altered her decisions had she known earlier? Would she regret her final choice after hearing everything her chosen said behind her back? Would she feel embarrassed about not having more self-respect when she sees how wishy-washy she was over red flags that were so big you could see them from the space station?

As much as I like to make sassy remarks as I watch the show about who should go home and how stupid she's being for keeping Luke P., the reality of the situation is that her train wreck was *my* train wreck. I was the one who had no self-respect and ignored red flags. In some respects, I was worse, because I *was* privy to some of the types of conversations that should make a person tuck tail and run.

At one point, I was in a relationship I had concerns over. I had fallen in love with a guy and had just made the big decision to sleep with him. At the time, I was just finding my way back to God. It wasn't long after we had started sleeping together when I was at a church service and felt Jesus asking me to walk down to the front to accept and receive Him as my Savior.

I will never forget sitting in that chair. My palms were sweaty and my legs were shaking. Embarrassment was sitting on me and Pride had me in a full-on head lock. I did *not* want to get up in front of *all those people* and walk to the *front* of the church. Besides, then they would all know I wasn't already saved. They'd all assume I was wallowing in sin prior to that very moment, and *that* would be embarrassing. But I wanted it. I wanted *Him*. In my heart of hearts I was ready and I asked God to give me the strength to stand up. That's it. Just. Stand. Up. The rest would fall into place if I could just do that. I realize this might sound weird and crazy, but I honestly remember standing to my feet by some means other than myself. It's a feeling I will never forget. And I mean, *never*. I knew it was Him. He wasn't forcing me. He was responding to my call for help. It was a beautiful moment.

Within a few days of that happening, I told the boy I was seeing that we needed to stop sleeping together. I felt convicted, and I knew sex outside of marriage was a sin. And now that I had asked Jesus into my heart, it suddenly felt more like an eighty-thousand-pound semi kind of sin. The boy was *not* happy. Not even a little. Despite claiming this faith for himself, he let me know, in no uncertain terms, and any chance he got, that he wasn't happy with *my* decision.

Red flag.

Ladies (or gentlemen), if you are in a relationship with someone who is pressuring you to have sex outside of marriage, and making you feel badly about it, run for the hills. Don't look back. Just run. That person has no respect for you or themselves, and their character is in serious question. If the two of you can't get on the same page with something like that, you'll have bigger and badder issues for the rest of your relationship or marriage. Yes, I know *badder* isn't a word, but this book wouldn't truly be mine unless I made up at least one word in it. (I'm sure there will be more.)

That was my concern. My red flag. But leaving that relationship wasn't easy, because I had a big problem. I was so in love with his family that I told myself it would get better. After losing my dad and having no relationship with my mom, I had latched onto things that felt like home, and I didn't want to grieve through another loss. I wasn't ready to grieve again so I stayed in that relationship, hoping and believing things would change.

This is going to be shocking for you, but things didn't change. I know, I know. It's so easy to see that from an outsider looking in, but when you're a messed-up kid who doesn't know which end is up, it's a lot harder. That relationship got a lot harder too, until eventually this person decided to give himself to someone else while he was still with me. Twice. And I don't mean twice with the same person. It took getting betrayed a second time before I finally ended that relationship.

My root of rejection grew an arm and a few legs.

On that note of rejection, I'd like to talk about something not a lot of people talk about. And if they do, they must be doing it very quietly. Do you want to know what else made me feel rejected in past relationships? Pornography.

I was in a serious relationship with a man who had a problem with pornography. I caught him with it, and he promised me he wouldn't look at that stuff anymore. A few weeks after that, I was using his computer, and attempted to copy and paste something I was doing in a Word document. I must not have copied it correctly, because when I did a Control-V, I got a *big* surprise in the middle of my document. I was sick to my stomach.

There are a lot of obvious reasons pornography is wrong. It corrupts and creates unhealthy desires (sex outside of marriage, sex with more than one person, sex that hurts someone, etc.). It enables those who are caught up in the sin of creating pornography. But it also devastates the significant other of the person addicted to it. Seeing him choose that hurt me more than I expected it to. In my mind, he wanted something that wasn't me. He was rejecting *me* and turning to someone else to fulfill his desires. Not only did it make me feel rejected, but inadequate. My body did *not* look like the bodies of those other girls. Did he find me so unattractive that he had to go to something that wasn't even real?

Speaking of what's not real, there was someone else I met who was very, well, charming. He said all the right things. He put my past worries at bay, and did everything possible to make me believe he was Mr. Right. Until that one time he didn't.

I was divorced at the time, and we had only been dating for a few months, but already I felt strongly for him. He seemed perfect. One evening we had gotten together with some of his extended family, and he drank a lot. More than I had ever seen him drink before. Toward the end of the evening, he decided it would be a good idea to make me the butt of every joke he was telling. That was embarrassing enough, but then he got nasty, and started berating me for being divorced, insinuating I was less than whole because of it. I remember leaving the room, walking outside, and just standing there in the cold, December air. I was so confused.

Confused was the last thing I should have been. I should have been clear. Very clear. No one who loves and respects you treats you that way. I shouldn't have stopped when I got to the driveway. Uber wasn't born yet, so I should have called a taxi and went home. But I didn't. I stood outside waiting. Wanting him to come out and apologize profusely to me. Wanting him to tell me why he was being such an ass and promise to never do it again. I winced just typing that. It's true that's what I felt at the time, but the woman I am today hardly has the stomach to even write that. It's glaringly obvious now how wrong I was, but time only moves forward.

By the time I went back inside, he was passed out on the couch. I slept in the guest room and tossed and turned until morning as Satan's lies encircled me. I *was* divorced. I *was* broken. Perhaps out of the overflow of the drunken heart the mouth speaks, and maybe it's truth.

When he finally roused himself from his drunken stupor, he did apologize to me. Profusely. Like the man who beats his wife, apologizes the next morning, and then does it again. Yes, he did it again. And again. And again. I stayed in that relationship because of lies I chose to believe about my circumstances and myself. Let's pull a few nose hairs and list some of them.

> *I'm divorced and that means I'm used goods.*
>
> *I'll never find a good, Christian man who is single.*
>
> *I'm not good when I'm alone.*
>
> *Most men won't want to date a woman with a child.*
>
> *All men cheat, so I might as well get used to it.*
>
> *If I wait too long, I won't be able to have any more kids.*

That last one is true, but it's never a reason to rush something so significant. At the heart of all these things is an ugly word. Insecurity. Uncertainty about yourself can cause reckless thinking which leads to reckless behavior. When your identify is rooted in anything other than Christ, it can lead you into valleys so low, you'll need scuba gear to deal with the pressure.

That relationship eventually ended, but not before it completely annihilated any shred of self-confidence I had. All I could see in the mirror was a small version of a once larger-than-life girl who used to know how to be happy even amidst the storms. That girl who was too ignorant to believe anything other than what her dad told her about being able to do anything. How disappointed he'd be to see me then. It had felt like acid rain was falling around me, only I was dissolving from the inside out.

These are just some of the examples of my time in the valley. We'll get into more of it shortly, but suffice it to say, the enemy was working overtime on me, and I let his lies continue to build and fester, melding themselves into the DNA of who I thought I was. Or, rather, what I thought I was worth.

In my hunger for acceptance, Pavlov's bell was ringing again, and it was ringing loudly. Only this time, Satan had me where he wanted me, and was ready to up the ante and go all in.

My cancer called rejection was about to escalate to stage four terminal.

Chapter 7

Hell on Earth

She lay on her bed, her pillow wet with tears that wouldn't cease. There were no words that could do her agony justice. The weight on her chest felt like an anvil, and the pit in her stomach grew with every difficult breath she tried to draw in. She cried out to God, wondering what she had done wrong. Or maybe it what was what she *hadn't* done that caused all of this. She felt sick to her stomach, and she could see no path forward. Grief overtook her as the images she was trying so hard to keep out clawed at her mind. They pried and forced their way in until the door was broken down and she lay pierced by its shards of wood. The waves of images flooded her like a tsunami, consuming her and throwing her every way but safe. She wanted to forgive. Could she? *Would* she?

This is how I see her. The woman whose husband I had an affair with. It wasn't always how I saw her, but it is now. After experiencing the raw end of unfaithfulness, I should have known better. I should have *done* better. But I didn't. I took something that didn't belong to me, and I can never fully give it back. And I did that all in the name of love, and the search for acceptance.

> "When tempted, no one should say, 'God is tempting me.' For God cannot be tempted by evil, nor does He tempt anyone; but each person is tempted when they are dragged away by their own evil desire and enticed. Then, after desire has conceived, it gives birth to sin; and sin, when it is full-grown, gives birth to death." James 1:13-15

The day I sat on my own bed, feeling not so unlike the woman who's heart I had shattered, I never would have believed it had you told me I would someday make a decision to be the other woman. But deadly sin can be insidious. It can build so slowly and innocuously that you hardly notice what's happening.

My book, *The Waiting Room*, is all about encouragement while we are waiting on the promises of God to manifest. It's filled with reminders of how our God has perfect timing and why it's so important to trust the plan He's already established. Satan learned that from God. He took a play out of God's book and learned to patiently wait. And watch.

> "Be alert and of sober mind. Your enemy the devil prowls around like a roaring lion looking for someone to devour." 1 Peter 5:8

Satan studies us. He watches us react to things, both good and bad. He sees our weaknesses and understands what triggers them. He hears the things we say to our friends and

Tell Them

the things we say when we think no one is listening. He hears us when we are crying out to God and laying bare the desires of our hearts.

He uses those desires against us.

Little by very little he puts opportunities in front of us, masquerading as our desires. But his version of them pose threats to our convictions. They are small at first. Barely recognizable. So small, that you tell yourself it isn't a big deal. Because in your mind it *isn't*.

You wake up one morning and take a hard look in the mirror. You hate that you're still single, and wonder if those awful things someone uncaring once said to you are true. You say to yourself,

"Maybe I'm not as attractive as I could be. Maybe I do need to lose a few pounds before a nice man will notice me long enough to see my personality." You sigh, finish getting ready, and go to work.

"You look nice today."

Well, thank you very much!

It feels good, doesn't it? When someone notices you during a time when you feel unattractive. Is it a coincidence that you were just lamenting over your looks this morning and then this nice man complimented you? This nice *married* man. Remember how Satan feeds on our weaknesses and tempts us with things masquerading as our desires? Remember how his temptations require us to compromise on our beliefs? You tell yourself that someone complimenting you is polite, not inappropriate, and that satisfies your conviction for the moment.

I promised you transparency, so after dropping the turd on the table about having an affair, I'm not going to wuss out now, because I'm hoping what I have to say can save someone else from the same decision. I'm hoping my transparency can help someone else to identify unhealthy thoughts and behaviors *before* they take root and destroy lives.

Saying this now makes me a little sick, because I hate that I was ever this person, but it's the foundation of truth for everything else. After going through some pretty rough relational hurricanes, my personal self-worth was at an all-time low. I was insecure. I was a single mom, and I was afraid that's exactly how I was going to stay. I was afraid I would never find a decent, Jesus-loving man, and I was also afraid I would never truly experience one of the deepest desires of my heart – to be cherished by someone. All the others had thrown me away. Some of them had even told me verbally how little I was worth.

When someone I knew to be decent and kind told me I looked nice, it stirred something in me that I had a choice to squelch and walk away from. But I didn't. Compliments to an insecure and desiring woman are like crack to a drug addict. It's a fix that leaves them wanting more.

It left *me* wanting more.

I found myself trying a little harder to look nice, and the compliments kept their steady stream. Soon, passing comments turned into unnecessary stops at each other's work station to talk for a few minutes about nothing important. Soon after that, there was the invitation to go to lunch with the group. Again, you find yourself at a crossroads. You tell yourself it isn't one-on-one, so it's fine. There will be adult supervision, so it's really not a big deal.

Stop right there.

Tell Them

The minute we start making excuses or justifying our actions to make us feel better about something is red flag numero uno. You're right. It's not a big deal.

It's a gigantic, life-altering, axis-tilting, magnetic pole reversing deal.

I talked myself through all of those little justifications. One by one, I told myself I could handle it, and I was just enjoying the attention. No one was getting hurt. But that's a lie. *Everyone* was getting hurt. Fire consumes. It may start out like a small spark, but it grows as it consumes what's around it, until it's out of control.

The surface temperature of the Sun is over 9,000 degrees Fahrenheit. Considering most pizza places send their pizzas though the conveyer belt at around 500 degrees Fahrenheit, we're talking about an 8,500-degree swing in quickly going from something pleasurable to something that would completely consume and obliterate. Which is exactly what happened.

Every decision I made to entertain and eventually get in bed with death, I made knowing I was compromising. I had opportunity after opportunity to shut it down, but I kept pressing the line. I kept rubbing my foot over it until there was no more line to see.

A big reason for rubbing that line away was because I developed feelings for this person. Curiosity turned to attraction which eventually turned to love, or what Satan made me believe was love. My compromise opened the door to create opportunity to spend time together.

Caroline Klug

When desire meets opportunity, it will either result in something wonderful, if it's God-centered, or something devastating if it's not.

Do you want to know the biggest lie I told myself while dancing with death? I told myself that because I wasn't with anyone, *I* wasn't the one cheating, and that made it better. Maybe not okay, but not *nearly* as bad. There are so many things wrong with that kind of thinking, I barely know where to start.

Sweet One, whether you're considering a waltz with demise or you're already in a full-on tango with the Reaper, I'm begging you to clear your precious and foolish head and keep reading. What I'm going to share, I share out of the deepest recesses of my heart. This next part is hard to relive, but it's necessary for me to heal, and potentially vital for you to live.

> "What benefit did you reap at the time from the things you are now ashamed of? Those things result in death!" Romans 6:21

It's a lie straight from the pit of hell to think something as noxious as an affair doesn't hurt people. Let's start with the person who feels the brunt of the betrayal – the significant other who finds themselves caught in the crossfire, usually with no warning and certainly wearing no protective gear. It's a devastating blow that shakes the core of everything they believe about love and trust.

I know, because I was there. More than once. I know what it feels like to try to disconnect from the rejection, betrayal, and haunting images of the person you love with

Tell Them

someone else. I know what it feels like to wonder what starting over even looks like, and all the worries and concerns that come bundled in with that atomic bomb of a mess. I know what it feels like to question everything about yourself and wonder why you're not enough. I know what it feels like to have people in your life torn from you, and watch your family and friends get dismantled all because of something you didn't even ask for.

I even know what it feels like to get an accidental butt dial from your significant other *while* they are with someone else, and you now have a front row seat to the conversation that confirms their infidelity.

Because I had front row seats to multiple shows, I had zero excuse for my behavior. I had zero excuse for the hurt I knowingly caused someone innocent.

That's not the only hurt we cause when we step into something like that. The person you're having an affair with is being ripped in two. I carried around an enormous amount of guilt and grief over that situation and I wasn't even with someone. I can't imagine the turmoil the person who was with someone else felt. Every single day they are living a lie in front of the very people who are trusting and depending on them to provide love and security. They are a walking falsehood with a reservoir of guilt so deep and so expansive, there's no way the dam they built can hold it all in. It's just a matter of time before the cracks start forming under the pressure. That pressure will eventually collapse the dam and send that water flooding and drowning everyone around them, including you.

Kids and extended family get hurt too. No, not hurt. Annihilated. Pummeled and drown by the water. In what world do the innocent kids associated with all parties involved deserve to be caught up in that mess? They are worse than blindsided. They are now forced to suffer the consequences of the fallout, whether it's a life-long tension between their parents or a complete upheaval of life as they know it because of divorce. The ramifications of such selfish behavior can have devastating impacts for generations to come.

Here's another lie:

"It's not my fault, because he isn't happy in his marriage and it was going to be over anyway."

It doesn't matter if the person you're with tells you they aren't happy. It doesn't matter if they tell you their marriage is already over. It's not over in God's eyes, and it certainly might not be over in the eyes of that person's spouse. This is an obvious but difficult truth:

You can't believe everything the person you're with is telling you.

It's true what they say that hurting people hurt people. So do selfish people. The heart wants what the heart wants, and that's usually at the expense of someone else. The person I was with told me they loved me and wanted to be with me, yet after every time we were together, he left to go back home to someone else. That is all kinds of messed up. Not only the part about him going home to someone else, but the part where I let him come back to me. If that's not the most flagrant display of self-hate and disrespect, I don't know what is. Take it from someone who's been there. Twice. It will never be worth it.

Tell Them

Yes, you read that right. Twice. It doesn't pay to go into the other one, because it looks the same as the one I just described. Take everything I just said about this devastating mess and multiply it by two. Same inputs. Same outputs. Same insecure woman looking for love and acceptance, and same catastrophic annihilation of self and others.

It doesn't matter what you've told yourself, or any of the reasons you've come up with to make yourself believe you deserve this. Yes, that's what I told myself. Both times. I told myself I *deserved* this relationship. Life *owed* me. I had suffered copious amounts of loss and been served a refrigerator full of shit sandwiches, and this was life repaying me with something I thought would make me happy, even at the expense of others. Others did it all the time, so why shouldn't I?

How ridiculous. How incredibly selfish, immature, and ridiculous. The only thing I deserved were all of the painful consequences that resulted from my choices.

Even if that person ends up leaving their spouse to marry you, you will never experience the true happiness and freedom that comes from something God-given. I'm not saying a marriage that starts under those conditions can't bring happiness or even that it can't eventually be God-centered. I'm only saying grace doesn't always eliminate the consequences. You will always have the knowledge of *how* you got together hanging over you. And if you chose to make up a different version, then you will always have the weight of your lies festering and growing inside of you like a painful disease. Always wondering when you'll be found out. Always anxious when those who know the real truth enter in and out of your life situations and threaten the fictional account you've worked so hard to maintain. If there are kids involved, you will always have the guilt of knowing the role you played in the trajectory of their lives spinning 180 degrees to the south. As for your new partner, you may have an underlying current of distrust between you, whether spoken or unspoken. After all, the person you're with cheated on their spouse to be with you. Who's to say they won't do it again to *you* when the weather gets a little stormy?

Another obvious target for destruction is *you*. Please hear me when I tell you there isn't any part of the consequences of that decision that won't leave you worse than the opportunity found you. Every moment you chose to spend in that situation is another moment you will be compromising your self-worth, and the negative feelings bound to consume you will torment you from the inside out. They will leave you feeling so little of yourself, that being someone's secret side dish will look deceptively attractive. And although it will come with so much emotional pain you can't see straight, you will tolerate it as you sell pieces of your soul, until there's nothing left. You will wake up one day and wonder how you got into the pit you can't get out of, let alone see the surface of. There will be nothing but darkness, and if you think I'm being dramatic, then wait until we talk about hell on earth. Because I haven't even gotten there yet.

> "Then He will say to those on His left, 'Depart from me, you who are cursed, into the eternal fire prepared for the devil and his angels.'" Matthew 25:41

The Bible tells us if we accept Jesus as Savior and Lord of our life, we will be able to enjoy eternity with Him in His

Tell Them

Kingdom. If not – if we chose the things of this world over Him – then we will be cast into hell with the devil and his fallen angels. As a Christ follower, I don't believe all the weeping and gnashing of teeth we're told we'd experience in hell is solely because of its unquenchable fire. I believe the worst and most painful consequence of being in hell is the eternal separation from God one will experience every moment of every second of their self-chosen eternity. At that point, any doubt that person had about God's existence will be laid bare and they will know the truth. They will probably even be haunted by every opportunity God sent their way to know Him and accept Him, and they will have to live with the knowledge of God, and being damned to eternal separation from Him.

When I made these poor choices, I already knew Jesus as my Savior. That's hard to say. That offers about a bazillion more reasons why I should have done better. But if it's taught me anything, it's taught me not to be too cocky in my standing, because anyone can fall.

Because of the knowledge and relationship I had with Jesus, my life of sin impacted me in ways outside of all the obvious feelings and challenges. The guilt of my choices left me feeling unable to spend time with God. He knew what I had done. What I was *doing*. Reading His Word only convicted me, which was inconvenient to my desires. Praising Him seemed like ingenuine lip service because of the wall I had put up between us. Talking about Him with friends seemed hypocritical because I wasn't practicing what I preached. It seemed easier to stop. Everything. I stopped reading the Bible. I stopped listening to Christian music. I stopped attending church. Everything I had once known and loved about Him had now become a muddy mess.

Caroline Klug

> "If any of you lacks wisdom, you should ask God, who gives generously to all without finding fault, and it will be given to you." James 1:5

God tells us we can come to Him if we're in need of wisdom. If we're stuck and we don't know what to do, we can come to Him. It doesn't matter what we've done. Rather than blaming and telling us how awful we're behaving, He gives wisdom and guidance. He gives these things generously. Satan wants us to think we can't go to God amidst our sin. Keeping us separated is his objective, with his ultimate goal being our death. But the truth is, it didn't matter what I had done or even what river of sin I might have currently been wading in. I could have and should have come to God and asked Him to show me the way. But I didn't. I chose to believe the lie that I couldn't.

Here's the worst part. I knew I needed God. I was hurting so badly from this awful situation I found myself in, but saw no way to His Throne. Satan successfully convinced me I was no longer worthy, and my spiritual world went dark. The separation felt scary and ugly. It felt like I was no longer standing on solid ground, but a high wire. I *knew* my Jesus. I *knew* who He was and what He had done for me. I *knew* the love it was possible to feel from Him, but I was ashamed.

More transparently, even if I could have shaken off that lie, I was completely consumed by my desires, and approaching the Throne didn't feel like an option. I knew God would ask me to give that relationship up, and I wasn't ready to let go.

But wait. Maybe I *could* have them both.

Tell Them

Are you ready for this one? Satan had me convinced I could endure this separation from God long enough to obtain my worldly desires, and then I'd just ask for forgiveness and everything would be okay. I could go back to singing praise songs in my car and getting excited about Hebrew and Greek root words in the Bible. It would be a mere blip on our spiritual timeline, and everything would be just as it should be.

Who was I kidding?

Yes, God is loving and forgiving and merciful, but He's not a fool. I couldn't play Him like a disconnected set of parents. And even if my heart did get right and my intentions for receiving forgiveness were pure, I'd still have to face the music of my consequences. There's no way I could expect everything would be washed over like it never happened. Had I gone forward in either of those relationships, forgiveness or not, I would have had all the fallout we talked about earlier.

That whole sin and forgive thing is a lie I'm ashamed to admit having believed, but it was my only plan. I knew I couldn't live without Jesus, and my flesh told me this was the only way to have the desires of my heart. I gambled with my soul and threw the dice.

When my daughter Kyra was first at the age of needing to hear about drugs, I told her drugs are dangerous and unpredictable. Just because the person offering it to you might have done it a hundred times with no visible consequences means nothing. Kids die from their first drug use all the time. I used an analogy with her I hoped would stick with her if she ever found herself being tempted. I told her doing drugs is like putting on a blindfold and walking across the highway. It's possible you can make it across without getting hit, but there's no guarantee. And just because your friend made it, doesn't mean you will. Sin is a lot like that. It's a gamble that could take your very life.

With each passing day, and each passing roll of the die, I could feel everything caving in on me. My blindfold made everything dark and I could hear the vehicles whizzing past me, some even brushing against my clothing. My worldly desires had such a stronghold on me, I could barely breathe.

You've just gotten a close look at one of two utterly catastrophic events, which are the bookends of a decade-long storm. Let's spend a few chapters looking more closely at what transpired during that decade of disaster.

Chapter 8
It's Not All Fetch & Treats

As you know from the earlier chapters, I struggled to make friends when I was younger because of how *different* I was. I was never accepted into any of the friend groups, and the only party invitations I ever got were from kids whose parents forced them to invite *all* the kids in class. My presence was a necessary evil if they wanted their party to happen. A normal kid would have thrown the invitations in the garbage. Not me. Every time I got invited, I went. I couldn't help but think *this* might be the time when they actually had fun with me, and we could put all this Scut Farkus behind us.

One of my better qualities is that I don't hold a grudge. As long as I feel there's been mutual resolution, I'm completely fine going from *I want to throat punch you,* to *hey, let's go get some pizza,* all in the span of five minutes. It serves me well in relationships, but there's another side that might not be so healthy. When you're an acceptance seeker, you have a tendency to gloss over your own best interest in favor of optimism. You want so badly to belong, that you keep touching the burner even though you already know it's red hot.

Looking back, going to those parties was never any fun for me or the kids who invited me, and I should have just stayed home. But my quality of optimism kept me accepting those invitations. I knew they had to give them to me, but my more optimistic side wanted so badly to believe they wanted to give me a chance and be my friend. I was more than open to letting bygones be bygones and reciprocating. More descriptively said, I was a Labrador Retriever.

I'm about to make you cringe, but hopefully only temporarily. For the longest time, I hated dogs. Big ones. Ankle biters. It didn't matter. I hated them all. But that's because I didn't trust them, and I was fearful around the bigger ones. When I was growing up, we had a German shepherd named Sam. Sam was primarily my dad's dog, but all the kids played with him and he was very well trained.

I was 6 years old when it happened. I was sitting on the living room floor next to Sam. My mom had brought him a porkchop bone and set it in front of him. I was told later Sam growled at me, but I hadn't heard him. I was too absorbed in whatever a 6-year-old does. I'm not sure why he got upset, but I assume he thought I was there to take his bone. What I do remember is the sound of a dog attacking. That sound is still burned in my memory, and sends shivers up my spine if I hear it on television or, God forbid, in person.

The moments that followed that horrible sound are still mostly a blur to me. It wasn't until I got into my twenties that I started having small pieces of that memory come back. The Pepto pink bath towel was my first piece of the puzzle.

Tell Them

The one being held against my face while I was rushed to the Emergency Room.

Sam was quite a large dog, and this 6-year-old runt of the litter was no match. Along with several other wounds, he had torn the right side of my mouth off. I was very lucky, in that his lower teeth punctured my neck just centimeters from my jugular. I have that scar to prove it.

Through odd circumstances, a specialty doctor, Dr. David Finch, a pioneer in cosmetic and reconstructive surgery, happened to be standing in the Emergency Room of St. Elizabeth's Hospital when he heard about a 6-year-old girl who had just been brought in after being mauled by a German shepherd.

He wasn't even supposed to be there that night, but he said he knew he was the guy to help this little girl save her face. He rolled up his sleeves and he went to work reconstructing my mouth and placing 187 stitches throughout my face and neck. Those wounds healed, and the scars were pretty red for a long time, which only contributed to why I dangled from the last rung of the middle school social ladder. Let's say it was another defining *difference* of mine.

As a Christian, I don't believe in coincidence. I believe in a God who has such mastery of control, that He is able to turn the chaos of every movement of every being and every creature into a symphony of glory. That renown plastic surgeon being in the right place at the right time wasn't a coincidence. It was a gift. It was a gift from the Father of heavenly lights. Think about the things you might have mistaken for coincidence, and imagine how God's hand could have been on that instead. You might be surprised what you find.

Since that time, I had always steered clear of dogs. Even my sisters' loving golden retrievers. It wasn't until I met Jim, who had a black lab and a rat terrier, that I softened to the idea. I never met his lab, April. She was 18 years old, and had passed away not long before we met. I did get to know his little rat terrier, Milo. Milo was 20 years old, and as sweet as sweet could be. He tendered himself into my heart very quickly. I'm sure Jim being part of that equation helped. After that, the light bulb went on. I didn't see dogs as mini monsters anymore. I saw them for what they are. They are loving creatures who want to love you as much as they want to *be* loved by you.

I realized I had found a kindred spirit. It was a revelation that helped me understand myself a little better. I was a Labrador retriever. They are outgoing, gentle, intelligent, and easy to train. They also love the heck out of you, and want to be loved back the same way. Loyalty runs deep with this breed, and they often live to please and serve their owners. They want so badly for you to love them, that even if you're not that nice to them, they just keep coming back and trying again. I had just found my identity in a dog breed.

Being a Labrador is not all fetch and treats. It's hard being so vulnerable. I wanted someone who would recognize the loyal partner they had and cherish me. I wasn't finding that in my relationships, but I was finding it in my career. In my mind, my personal and professional lives were being accessed on dangerously different scales. I saw myself as unloved and unworthy on the personal side, and thought my professional success was all that made me valuable. So that's where I focused.

After I graduated from the University of Wisconsin Oshkosh, I started out as a web application developer, creating company intranet sites, when that was a new and hot functionality. I was promoted to a business analyst, and then fell into project management kind of by accident.

I fell, all right. I fell in *love*. This was my kind of job. Building plans, managing timelines, and hitting aggressive business goals. I got to work with different teams of people, and projects were always changing. I felt like a little kid in a candy shop. I was promoted to a program manager, and then portfolio manager, and had the opportunity to work closely with senior leadership in building and executing strategic objectives. I'm a big-picture person, so this was right up my alley. I was in my happy place because I was good at it.

I found my career was not so dissimilar from high school Forensics. With hard work and diligence, I could tackle whatever I put my mind to. It was about memorizing my piece (being an expert in my area). It was about learning the blocking (where to be at the right time). It was also about knowing my audience (understanding what leaders were looking for). I figured out what they were most interested in and, because I'm a Labrador, I chased down that ball and brought it back to them. Every time. I became known for my consistency of performance and those two, shiny words that seemed to show up on every performance review I've ever received. Results Driver. Those words were like music to my ears. They were especially fine when accompanied by a smiling boss and a bonus check. More treats and a belly rub. It meant my owners were happy, and that meant I was performing well, and *that* meant I was valuable. Pavlov's dog was one happy mutt, and that bell was ringing like the Salvation Army during Christmas season.

> "For they loved human praise more than praise from God." John 12:43

I rode that roller coaster for a long time. I would spend my days getting built up, riding high on the accolades. Then I would come home and my roller coaster would dive down through the dark tunnel. It was relentless, but for some reason I kept buying tickets. Why do addicts do anything? Because it makes them feel good. Because whatever they're receiving is making them feel better than what they're getting from the world as they know it. I felt good about myself when I was at work, because others told me I was appreciated. Forget the fact that those types of praises are completely conditional. I didn't care. I just wanted to hear them. I *needed* to hear them, so I worked hard to ensure I would. I tolerated the tunnels because I loved coming out of them. I just hadn't figured out how to *stay* out of them. I hadn't figured out how to take the spirit of what I was learning at work and apply it to my personal life. Not the part where I had an unhealthy response to praise, but the part that showed me I was an intelligent and capable woman, and that didn't stop when I crossed the threshold from work to home.

Having a Labrador personality can be especially difficult when it comes to friendships. We want to love and be loved, and we'll often do tricks to make that happen. Whenever I felt like I wasn't getting played with enough, I gravitated to the comfort of my work life and made it about performance.

Tell Them

I was always the one scheduling the get-togethers and doing all the planning. I *do* love to plan, and I only do it now if I want to, but back then, I did it out of fear of people forgetting about me. Because I worried I was forgettable. If I suggested and planned events, then I wouldn't have to sit on my couch watching re-runs of Forensics Files. It's hard to watch all the Facebook posts come through of your friends doing fun things together. *Without you.* Sitting on that couch felt like sitting in the warming well on the middle school playground all over again.

Before I got comfortable in my own skin, I really struggled with loneliness. As an extrovert, I draw energy from being around others. As a crutch, I started leaving the television on in the background during the evenings or weekends, while I did whatever else I was doing. I found it made the place feel not so empty. To this day, I still have that bad habit of leaving the television on. It's on right now as I'm writing this. The Science Channel, in case you're wondering. It's usually either that or HGTV. Love me some *Fixer Upper.*

Why the loneliness and victim thinking? The search for acceptance, of course. It always seems to come back to that. When it comes to friendships, my need for acceptance, coupled with my natural drive, can lead me to a lot of one-sided effort. I have a tendency to give a lot of myself, but if that give isn't returned, it can leave me feeling, once again, rejected. It makes me feel like I'm always doing everything for everyone else and no one is doing anything for me. I get how pathetic that sounds, but it's true. Especially for single moms. After being one so long, I can tell you this is a real issue.

Caroline Klug

I sometimes struggle with feeling as though the people around me either take me for granted or they take advantage of me, because they know, or assume, I'll handle things. *Because I usually do.* Always being the one to do everything gets exhausting, and it only exacerbates whatever negative emotions I was already feeling. I've grown in this area, but I'm still susceptible to the lie when I'm feeling overwhelmed.

In the past, my answer to that would have been to simply *try harder.* Now, I know that kind of victim thinking is a lie, and I just spend a little time grounding myself in the truth – whether that's Scripture or just the plain, simple truth that there are a *lot* of people in my life who love me and care about me. I am truly blessed.

At the end of the day, people want to know they matter. To someone. Anyone. They want to know they are valued and would be missed if not accounted for.

The hard truth is, in the past, I often felt unaccounted for. There were a few people who checked in on me now and then, but I was missing an inner circle. My tribe. I was missing the people who would miss *me*, and I didn't want to feel alone anymore. I wanted to feel loved. But the Labrador in me just kept trying. I kept thinking it was about what I *did* versus who I *was.* It landed me in a cycle of rinse and repeat. And the machine was set to cold water.

After a while, I got frustrated. And a while after that, I got angry. That cycle had a tendency to push my justice button.

Chapter 9
Your Blinker Isn't for You

I can be a very rule-oriented individual. Whether it's a natural law of the universe or simply a sign that says, "Please don't taunt the monkeys," I obey it. I figure there's a *reason* someone went through all the trouble of creating it in the first place.

When monkeys are in captivity, they can get very stressed and agitated. When experiencing stressors, they have a natural inclination to throw things. When they're in a cage, there's really not a lot of options to pick from when little Johnny comes up and starts screaming at the top of his precious little lungs. There's really only one easily accessible and free-standing projectile within reach. Fecal matter.

Until you've graduated through the hazing of the fifth-grade trip to the zoo, when you're forced by your peers to agitate the monkeys, you have no idea that when monkeys get upset, they throw their poop at you. Hence, the sign not to taunt the monkeys, and a logical addition into the natural lawbook of the universe. (Also, a good candidate for an eleventh commandment, if God so chooses.) In my mind, rules

Caroline Klug

are meant to keep us in our lanes and protect us from getting into life's otherwise avoidable accidents.

In the matter of driving, one of my big rule-breaking pet peeves is when people don't use their blinkers. Blinkers were born out of the same mess as projectile monkey poop. It's the equivalent of a sign that says, "Please don't taunt the other drivers." If drivers don't get the appropriate forewarning of which direction your car is going in, then the odds of having an accident greatly increase. If I know you are about to merge into the center lane of a busy three-lane highway, then I will wait until you have safely arrived and ensure proper distance behind you before completing *my* merge. When it's my turn, I check traffic (flashback to Driver's Ed: blinker, mirror, blind spot) and responsibly flip my blinker on.

Hey everyone! I'm about to merge right! Everyone see what I'm about to do? Okay, great! Here I go!

Only after I arrive safely in my designated lane do I turn off my blinker. Driving doesn't always happen that way. Sometimes we do the right thing, use our blinkers, and there's still someone who decides to recklessly cruise into the middle lane a second before you do, without any thought to using their blinker to announce their rudeness. This causes unnecessary mayhem, as well as a few choice words I don't always have the restraint to hold back on (another confession).

Another one that bugs me is four-way stops. As cars roll up to their respective stop signs, each car moves through the intersection, one at a time, in the order by which they first arrived. Seems pretty basic, right? Some young and eager traffic engineer spent a lot of time thinking that one through. We owe it to that person, as a matter of civic duty, to carry out that brilliant facilitation. I might think it's brilliant because it's *fair*. Seems only right that the person who got there first should get to go first. But there's always *that guy* who gets to the intersection after you, who feels he can take it upon himself to change the rules. You hit your brakes with your nose already in the intersection as he burns through it in front of you.

Not cool, man, not cool.

I really hate when other people don't follow the rules. It pushes my imaginary justice button. I'm not sure what chemical reaction is being set off in my brain, but when others around me don't play by the socially accepted rules, I get very agitated, and, in some cases, downright angry. Although I can get triggered by the hard and fast rules like those for driving, it really comes more into play for me when it comes to basic human behavior and how people are treated.

This justice button began developing in me at a very early age. If we rewind to those hours I spent sitting on the bleachers in the gymnasium of my middle school, watching the other kids play games I couldn't, we see it start there. Yes, I was mad at the world for being *different*, but what made me really angry was the taunting from the other kids for not being able to participate. As if I'd rather work on my under-the-bleacher gum wad collection (sorry, janitorial staff).

Hey moron, you do realize this isn't exactly a choice for me, right? You do realize I'd much rather be out there whacking that whiffle ball into your forehead, right?

Again, I hold no animosity today for any of those kids. I don't expect they had the emotional maturity at the time to seek understanding. It was a bully or be bullied mentality, and the transparency of my differences just happened to land me on the wrong side too quickly to recover.

As a side note, there were a few of these individuals who reached out to me as an adult to apologize for the way they had treated me. I was very touched by that, and felt genuinely appreciative of their bravery and humility. As far as I'm concerned, it's water under the bridge, and it was just another piece of the cosmic puzzle that made me who I am today.

As you know, I made it through the middle school madness and graduated to a happier high school experience. Life was, I would wager to say, exceptional from a school and social standpoint. I spent the day feeling loved and accepted by my friends, teachers, and extracurricular coaches. My theater nickname was Bubbles, because I was always so happy and bubbly. Gratitude has never been lost on me. When you go from living a life on the bleachers to doing high school dance team routines *for* the people on the bleachers, you have a tendency to appreciate the change in scenery.

I wish I could say I was looking at that same beautiful view all the time, but there was a relationship that was very critical to my childhood development that was very much lacking. This important person in my life was physically present, but emotionally disconnected. Disconnected is actually a polite word. When people in your life who are supposed to love you unconditionally tell you they hate you, wish you had never been born, and blame their financial hardships on you (because of my health condition), it has a tendency to leave a very deep wound. One that rears its ugly head for a very long time, and in the most inopportune of ways.

Tell Them

Processing rejection from someone close to you, as an adult, is hard. Processing that same rejection as a child is devastating. It's confusing and contrary to everything social norms teach you, and the feeling of abandonment lingers like the stink from a septic tank. Because it was so contradictory, not only did it pile on the injustice I felt, like turpentine on an open wound, but it also fed the feelings of brokenness. For how could someone who, by all rules of nature *had* to love you, actually hate you instead? Although I had others in my life who sent the opposite message with their love and emotional investment, it was hard not to focus on the part that was broken. Which made *me* feel broken.

When we're in the middle of injustice, it's difficult to fully recognize that it's not us who are broken, but the one who is *doing* the hurting.

As an adult, I now recognize that hurting people hurt people. Even if I could go back, I don't know if there's anything I could have changed about the situation, but what I do have the opportunity to do – what *you* have the opportunity to do with the injustices in your own life – is have the self-confidence not to let someone else tell you what you're worth. Forgive them, and allow the experience to make you a better person. I know I just made that sound easy. It's definitely not – especially when it's a relationship that's close to you, and processing their rejection is confusing. You just have to keep reminding yourself that it's not about you. It's about them. They need help, and most of all, they need love and acceptance themselves.

In the spirit of maintaining full transparency and honesty with you, I'll tell you that today, as a grown adult, I'm still struggling with how to address this specific relationship. Sometimes it's easier to pretend something doesn't exist than it is to go through the pain of digging up the bones and dealing with reality. God has definitely been talking me through this one as of late. The process of writing this book is causing my heart to soften, and I'm going to make a new attempt to forgive and find common ground. I'm sure it won't be easy for either of us, but I would be a hypocrite if I didn't at least try, right? You have my word, here and now, that I will try. God will have to direct my steps on what that looks like, but I will do what He asks of me, even if it's hard. If there's an estranged relationship in your life that God has been talking to you about, I hope you will consider doing the same.

Speaking of hard, after my dad died, we were unable to have any of his personal possessions. I won't go into any of that here, but it was a very difficult time for us and, on top of the grieving we were already doing, it felt like a lot of injustice. I decided to take matters into my own hands. Quite literally. When no one else was home, I stole my dad's Bible and the blanket he used in his recliner. They were the two things I saw him with every morning, without fail. I hid them away and I still have them both today. I'm sure we could make the argument that what I did wasn't awful, and it was done with loving intention of having something special of his. But the truth is, those things were not mine to take. I also took something that wasn't even his. And I did *that* out of spite.

God is good at using our poor choices to speak to us and guide us down a better path. I actually wonder if God is looking down on us sometimes, smiling as we do something, knowing full well He's going to bring it back around and use it to change us in ways we don't expect or even think we want. This particular incident involved the theft of a stainless-steel mixing bowl. It was the only one in the house, and it was used almost daily.

The Bible tells us we are made in God's image (Genesis 1:27). I have a healthy sense of humor, ergo, God has a healthy sense of humor. I still have that mixing bowl. Every time I pull it out, it makes me think of someone who abandoned me. No, it *forces* me to think about someone who abandoned me. Sometimes I feel angry, sometimes I feel sad, and sometimes I wonder if it could ever be different. *Was it too late to change the script?* Sometimes I wouldn't even use it and I'd grab a different one because I wanted to avoid thinking of that person all together. By my own making, what I intended to use to hurt someone, as childish as it seems, is the very object God has been using to keep that relationship in my mind and keep me open to wondering.

Loved One, we all hold onto things that don't belong to us – objects or emotions – but God can use all of it to work His guidance in our lives, if we are open to His leading.

There are other types of common injustice. Back to kitchen equipment: one of the benefits of being burned is learning how to recognize a hot burner. Because of what I experienced in a past relationship with being frequently manipulated, I now recognize it very quickly, and usually go to great lengths to avoid people like that. But what happens when avoidance isn't an option?

Caroline Klug

Sometimes God puts people in our path to help us grow from something we might have failed to properly navigate in our past. It's a new opportunity to respond differently, in a healthier, more Christ-loving way than we might have before. We can get mad because we have to deal with it, or we can look at it as an opportunity to destroy the control it has over us. Maybe we could even look at it as an opportunity to help that person by showing them undeserved mercy and love rather than judgement. Injustice is a difficult thing to navigate emotionally, but taking things into our own hands never bodes well.

Growing up the youngest of seven kids meant taking some teasing from them now and then. They were never allowed to upset me when my parents were around, out of fear of my having a tachycardic episode. But when Mom and Dad weren't around, they were pretty normal siblings. One afternoon, I was in the front yard with a few of my sisters, and was getting upset with them for teasing me. Of course, I told them to stop and, of course, they didn't. I was so angry at them, I started scouring the landscape for anything I could use to right this wrong. (It's a good thing for them we weren't a bunch of monkeys in a cage.)

I found an old straw laying in the road. Then, as if hand delivered by the Supreme Court, I saw it. A shriveled up and disgusting worm. Clearly dead. I picked up its sacrificial corpse, gave thanks, and shoved it in the straw.

Now, I'd like to preface this next part with acknowledging I wasn't exactly the sharpest tool in the shed when I was 8. Common sense must have eluded me during times of intense anger. I shoved that nasty worm in the dirty straw. In the most authoritative voice I could conjure up, I conveyed the threat that, should they not immediately cease

Tell Them

and desist, I would blow that nasty, dirty worm at them. Then I shoved the filthy straw in my mouth, and waited in the ready position. I remember them looking at me and laughing. *They did not cease and desist.* I had no choice. I had to neutralize the situation with force. I took in the biggest breath I could to ensure maximum velocity of the corpse.

I still had the straw pursed between my lips when I took in that gigantic breath.

I remember my sisters laughing hysterically as I dropped the straw and ran into the house in horror, my hands fixed dramatically around my neck, screaming, "I swallowed a worm! I swallowed a worm!"

My dad took one look at me, winced, and then told my brother to give me a glass of milk. At the time, I was horrified at his response. Later in life, I benefited from his solid wisdom, by giving Kyra milk after she ate a fly. Willingly. But that's a story for another time.

> "Do not take revenge, my dear friends, but leave room for God's wrath, for it is written: 'It is Mine to avenge; I will repay,' says the Lord." Romans 12:19

When we try to be someone else's Holy Spirit and take matters of spiritual justice into our own hands, we'll swallow dirty, shriveled up worm corpses. We need to leave room for God to do what only He can, in only the way He can. He sees the bigger picture, and He knows the perfect way and timing to guide and discipline His children. It never works out as well if we try to be the judge and jury. Speaking from personal experience, all that seems to do is stoke the angry flames. It's hard, but if you can learn to give these things to God, there's a supernatural peace that will follow. And if we're *really* spiritually maturing, we'll even ask God what we can learn from that situation.

Growth is good but, like the video games I'm horrible at, just when you think you've conquered a level, a new, more difficult, one is introduced. In Chapter 8, I mentioned I'm good at not holding grudges as long as there's mutual resolution. But if someone's not owning up to their role in the situation, well, that's a whole different game rating. Like the time someone cheated on me, denied it, and then started telling people *I* was the one who cheated. *Oo oo wait.* Someone definitely wasn't following the rules again.

What do people who have done something wrong and are confronted have a tendency to do? They lie. Again and again. We are mostly wired for self-preservation, and the worse the offense, the more the tendency to hide and bury those bones. When this happened, I didn't just want to hit the justice button. I wanted to body slam it. *How dare he! How dare he cheat on me and then tell people it was me!* I was outraged. That lie was hurting people I cared about and it was hurting me. I was so full of anger and hate my eyeballs were floating.

I ranted about it for a few days, trying to decide how I was going to handle this situation, because of course *I* had to handle it. I know God dislikes when I get all jacked up about injustice, because I usually try to take things into my own hands. I let His conviction fall on me and, in a moment of clarity, imagined Him in the facepalm position. I also imagined Him asking me, "Remember the worm corpse?" The still small voice of wisdom.

Tell Them

"In your anger do not sin: Do not let the sun go down while you are still angry, and do not give the devil a foothold .... Get rid of all bitterness, rage and anger, brawling and slander, along with every form of malice. Be kind and compassionate to one another, forgiving each other, just as in Christ God forgave you." Ephesians 4:26, 31-32

People need to follow the rules and use their blinkers. Otherwise, we don't know what they're going to do and we can be surprised by the direction they go. This person who lied about me didn't use their blinker, and it caused a giant accident, and a lot of people were injured.

The right thing is to follow what Ephesians 4 is telling us and forgive. But sometimes, when enough people burn through the intersection out of turn, it starts to break something in you. When enough rules are broken, it starts to make the rule keeper want to throw their arms up and join the party. I was tired. I was tired of seeing everyone else around me breaking the rules, and I was tired of doing the right thing and reaping none of the benefit I saw my enemies reaping. Satan was working on me again, and it was just a matter of time before I snapped.

Caroline Klug

Chapter 10
The Ghost of Christmas Past

When I was pregnant with Kyra, an unwelcome visitor arrived. I wasn't expecting it, and I certainly wasn't happy about it. I recognized it immediately by the familiar and dreaded sensation. I could always feel it in my lips first. They would start tingling a bit and turn a purply-blue color. That meant my circulation was off, which meant my heart was beating too fast for the small amount of oxygen I was taking in. My heart issues were back.

Up to this point, I had enjoyed almost ten blissful years of physical normalcy, but that party was over. All the fun had packed up and left, and I was now back to looming over my activities like a middle school hall monitor. By this point, medical advances had yielded me medication to control my condition, but there were certain stressors that could still trigger an episode. For instance, forcing your heart to beat for two people instead of one.

Intense heat was another thing my heart wasn't friends with. Couple being seven months prego with the high heat of August, and you have yourself an extravaganza of episodes. Whatever bliss I had enjoyed was now being pushed aside, as ten seasons of E.R. all rallied for air time. Doctors were worried about how I would handle the remaining term of my pregnancy and stress of labor, but with care and a lot of prayer, we both lived to tell the tale.

It got a little easier after Kyra was born. Until it didn't.

It was years later when the party came back. Except this time, it wasn't a good party. You told your parents it would only be a few friends. Now, you're standing on the second-floor landing, and can see your parents pulling in the driveway as you're staring at a few hundred kids, a tapped barrel of cheap beer, and... *oh my God, what are those two doing?* Brace for impact.

My heart issues had returned, along with a few new inconveniences. In addition to having episodes of it beating too fast, I started experiencing the opposite of it not beating fast enough to match my activity. To say this felt uncomfortable is an understatement. We lived in a duplex at the time, and all the bedrooms were upstairs. There were many times I recall walking slowly up the stairs, having to sit down on my bed once I got up there, and wondering if I might pass out and never wake up.

Rewind to when my dad passed away. That time period was one of the only exceptions to my blissful normalcy, as I had experienced a few episodes while dealing with the grief of his death. At the time, I went to see my cardiologist, where he did a full examination with testing. At the time, he mentioned an electrophysiologist (say that five times fast) who was traveling around the world perfecting a surgery he thought would be ideal for my condition, but it wasn't safe yet. He thought it might be ready in ten years or so.

Fast forward back to sitting on my bed and worrying about not waking up. I had scheduled another check-up

Tell Them

with my cardiologist to get some answers. That's when I found out the electrophysiologist I had heard about ten years earlier was now in my backyard, performing the very procedure that could help me. My doctor promised to send my files over to him, and I was elated. Elation quickly turned to devastation when he told me not to expect to get in to see him for at least six months.

My next stop was an attorney's office, where I had my first will drawn up. Based on what I was feeling, six months sounded like a long time. I was beginning to think it was a very real possibility something would happen to me, and I wanted to make sure Kyra would be taken care of. I didn't tell anyone else what was going on. I really don't know why. I was grieving the end of a relationship and maybe part of me just didn't want to open any more floodgates. If I talked about it, that would make it real. And I really couldn't deal with any more *real* at that point.

Remember the verbally abusive man who ridiculed me in front of my in-laws? The one who annihilated my self-confidence? That was the relationship that had just ended. One could offer the obvious observation that I should have bellied up to the barrel of cheap beer and celebrated. But hurt, broken people don't celebrate when unhealthy relationships end. They grieve. But the greater truth is, getting over the loss of that relationship wasn't the hard part. Yes, it felt like another tally in the long list of failures, and that was hard, but the really hard part was needing to heal from all of the bad that happened *during* it.

No one wakes up one morning and thinks, *golly gee whiz, I think I'm going to let someone verbally berate me today, and then let them do it again tomorrow.* Just like the dangers of sin, allowing yourself to be the object of abuse can creep in slowly over time. It's easy for others to call out when your bruises are on the outside, but what do you do when they are hidden on the inside, where no one can see them? That's where mine were. This man never hit me, but I sometimes wonder if that would have left me with less scars than his verbal method of abuse.

He was an alcoholic, a gambler, and addicted to prescription pain killers. I know this is going to sound hard to believe, but I had *no* idea. Not until it was too late. Not until the damage had already been done, both mentally and financially. I knew he drank a lot, but I had no idea just how much of a problem it was. I had no idea he took out new credit cards to pay off the old ones to hide the gambling debt. I had no idea when he drank one beer, he was really drinking six, because he later admitted he had no self-control to leave the rest of the six-pack behind. I had no idea he visited multiple doctors for fake injuries to get pain killers. And I certainly didn't know he was taking those pain killers while he was drinking all that beer. Why didn't I know?

Because he was hardly ever with me. The upswing to that was that he never interacted with Kyra much at all. At first that made me sad, but once I started experiencing the darker side of his behavior, I was relieved she had no exposure to that. When he did come around, it was always late, after she was in bed.

That usually meant it was between 2:00 a.m. and 3:00 a.m., he would be drunk, and was about to stagger up the steps and make a mess of my emotional well-being. I tensed up and braced for impact. It was the worst when he was drunk. That's when he would say the things he would later, in a sober-ish state, deny ever saying. That's when he would say the things so personal and hurtful it was almost impossible not to feel ugly. Repetition has a funny way of training us for the good or the bad. When you hear something enough times, and for long enough, you start to believe it.

I'm going to share some very intimate details. Not because I'm trying to be gratuitous, but because I think they might help someone else to understand their own potential situation. When a man takes prescription strength pain killers, especially when coupled with alcohol, that severely limits, if not completely prevents, him from getting or keeping an erection. Before I knew what he was taking, I went through a long period of time where he would want to have sex, but wouldn't be able to. His response was to tell me how I was the reason he wasn't able to. How I couldn't excite him because I wasn't attractive. But it wasn't enough to make it about me. He had to tell me about all the other girls who were able to get him excited. Those moments were a hell I wish on no one.

The manipulation was unparalleled. Had I not been so hurt by it, I might compliment him on his outstanding manipulative achievements. Never have I ever met someone with so much natural talent. When I finally did find out about the pain killers, and how he was acquiring them, naturally, I confronted him. By the time that conversation was over, he had me apologizing to him for snooping in his business. It wasn't until hours later that I realized I had just gone for a spin on the carnival ride. That ride was making me nauseous, and I wanted to get off.

Here's the really sick part. Even *after* I knew about the drugs, and the effects of them, I still allowed every bad thought he conditioned in me to survive and thrive. Even though I had the type of scientific explanation that would normally satiate my inquiring mind, I *still* believed all the lies. Conditioning is very hard to undo, and takes intentional discipline.

Eventually, my questions got too much and it was easier for him to start over fresh. He moved in with someone else and our relationship was over, but so was my hope. My stage four cancer called rejection had finally taken its toll, and I was admitted to spiritual hospice. I had no self-worth, I struggled every day with my warped perception of my physical appearance, and my heart was broken, both figuratively and physically.

That's when God burned another sentence on that neon sign. I felt completely and totally defeated when it happened. I was sitting on my living room couch when I heard Him.

"You can fall apart and let this break you, or you can fall on your knees and praise Me in your storm."

The moment of strength I found can only be explained by Grace, who was surely at my side. I slid off the couch and onto my knees. I had the Christian radio station on at the time, and a song began playing that will forever be burned in my heart – "Praise You in This Storm," by Casting Crowns. I sang. I cried. I even laughed.

In the few days that followed, something else happened. Something that would change things for me both figuratively *and* physically.

"I will give you a new heart and put a new spirit in you; I will remove from you your heart of stone and give you a heart of flesh." Ezekiel 36:26

Tell Them

The phone rang. My totally hip, cranberry red Motorola RAZR. I was about to learn that "Hello Moto" would never sound so beautiful. It was the receptionist at the office of the electrophysiologist. The one I was told I wouldn't hear from for at least six months. It had only been two weeks, so I wondered if this might just be another disappointing butt dial.

Nope. It was the real deal. The doctor's team had received my file, looked it over, and thought I fit the patient profile for their procedure perfectly. Sorry, that was a lot of P's, but the important thing to note is there would be no long line at Starbucks. There would be no Black Friday line outside Best Buy. There would be no more waiting. They wanted to see me, and asked if I could come in *that week*. The term "asses and elbows" might be a good description for my reaction to that question. *What? You need me to drive to Florida, take a slow-moving cargo ship to Antarctica, and then hang glide to Madagascar? Yeah, sure, I can clear my schedule for that.*

Within two weeks from that call, I had seen the doctor and been scheduled for surgery. The night before my surgery, when I was praising God for His help, God pressed that Scripture from Ezekiel on my heart. It's obvious how I would connect that to my surgery, getting a *new* heart and all, but He also spoke some things to me I wasn't completely prepared for. Like The Ghost of Christmas Past, He brought me back to those days in middle school, and He showed me *that* was where my root of rejection began. Like a children's red View Master classic, I saw reels of pictures go by of times in my life where that root grew and wrapped around me.

The surgery that next morning would be seven hours long and involve a double ablation. First, they would spend about three hours mapping all the electrical circuitry of my heart. They would map out all the pathways and identify where those electrical impulses were getting caught in a round-a-bout. Then, using a cold fusion technology, they would burn away the path to the two areas that didn't work right, forcing the electrical impulses to bypass the road under construction and go down a better, open road.

Even though I was poised to have this work done on my physical heart, God had His own surgery in mind.

Loved One, did you know God is better at fixing hearts than any earthly surgeon could ever dream of being? Did you know God can make your heart beat to a healthier drum by stopping the path to the bad places and creating new paths to the good places?

During the surgery, there was a tube inserted in my chest wall which they used to run the electrode wiring into my heart. Those wires were connected to a computer and literally controlled how fast my heart was beating. They would slow it down and speed it up. In fact, I understand during the surgery they had my heart over 200 beats per minute. That's mighty fast! That process was how they were able to map the natural path of the electrical impulses and find the trouble areas.

I think sometimes God allows the things of this world to speed up our hearts, so we can observe how we respond and find our trouble spots. We would never identify the areas we need to grow in unless we knew what triggered the reactions that did not make us the healthiest version of ourselves.

Tell Them

Once my operation was complete, the surgeon would need to re-test my heart function, to ensure they found all the bad pathways. Unfortunately, in order to do that, they had to leave the tube in my chest overnight, so they could put the wires back in the next day. That night was extremely difficult. I was sick from the anesthetic, and because that tube was still in my chest, any type of movement created sharp chest pains. I remember lying as still as I could, trying not to move, cough, or breathe too hard. In my mind, throwing up from the nausea just wouldn't be an option. Time passed like a Wisconsin cheese curd-hampered bowel movement. For the next three hours, I closed my eyes and breathed as shallowly as I could. I couldn't speak or move. It was the only way to keep the vomit down.

The Bible tells us we sometimes entertain angels unaware (Hebrews 13:2). Although she wasn't a heavenly angel, God sent an earthly angel to get me through those horrible hours. She was a friend I had somewhat lost contact with during that time in my life. I honestly have no recollection of how she found out about my surgery, but she showed up that night. She knew I couldn't visit, talk, or even open my eyes to acknowledge her presence, but she sat down anyway. She sat down, held my hand, and she prayed. For *three* hours. I'm sorry, but that's like superhero stuff. The last time I spent three solid hours in prayer was probably in the bathroom, after deciding a large ice cream shake would be a good way to celebrate the completion of a forty-day fast.

Moments after she let go of my hand and walked out the door, my eyes were open, and the nausea had passed. I recall the nurse coming in and saying, "Oh, you look so much better. We were so worried about you."

Yeah, I was worried about me too. I was able to sit up and drink some broth. Seems like a small thing, but that beef broth might as well have been a New York strip steak.

The next morning, they took me back into the surgery center to do the re-testing. I'm glad they didn't tell me the night before that I'd have to be fully alert when they do it. That meant no dreamland and not even any mild sedation.

Can I have a glass of red wine? No?

Having wires snaked through a tube and into your heart while you're awake is something they must have room for on *America's Got Talent*. I'm certain I would get at least one audience gasp. It was uncomfortable and terrifying.

For the next couple of hours, I laid as still as I could while they used their machine to slow down and speed up my heart, checking all the new pathways. One of the nurses on the surgical team must have saw the tears rolling down my cheeks, because she grabbed and held on to my hand. The whole time. Whenever the doctor needed something, if it required the opposite hand, she would first switch which hand was holding mine, and *then* she would do what he asked. What an incredible act of care and compassion.

Don't ever assume that just because you don't see, hear, or feel God personally that He isn't there and working on your behalf. Those people who come in and out of our lives – some for a long time and others for three hours – are His agents delivering a precious message that you are loved and cared for. My friend and that surgical nurse might have been holding my hand while I lay hurting and afraid, but so was Jesus. We need to look for and acknowledge those people

Tell Them

He uses to bring us comfort and answers to prayer, but we also need to be open to opportunities for God to use *our* hands to deliver those needed love letters to others.

A difficult part of the whole process for me turned out to be the emotions I struggled with after the surgery. I was living alone at the time, so my sister, Suzy, insisted I stay at her house for a few days while I recovered, and that was a nice blessing. She's thoughtful and mothering that way. Physically, I was a little uncomfortable, and my chest was sore, but it was a pretty minor discomfort overall. What wasn't minor were the emotions I found myself wrestling with. I felt like someone had thrown me in a foxhole, shot heavy artillery over my head all night, and then made me crawl out while the shooting was still going on. I was a mess. I was anxious, sad, and angry all rolled into one. And I cried for unknown reasons. Suzy handed me a bagel with my favorite pear jam on it and I cried. I had no idea what was going on with me. This lasted for three days.

Then I found out about something called surgical stress response. Without going into a lot of scientific mumbo jumbo, I'll try to sum it up as the nervous system sending signals from the injured site (my heart) to my hypothalamus. My brain thought I was under fire, so it activated all my stress responses. That sounded ridiculous to me, because here I was, feeling perfectly fine physically. In fact, I had myself a refurbished heart, and life was great. My first inclination was to push past it, but after praying about it, I started dissecting what happened a little.

Twenty-seven.

That's how many things I counted got poked, prodded, or inserted into my body during my operations. It wasn't

Caroline Klug

until I acknowledged what I went through to get to this good spot, without belittling it, that I suddenly found some peace.

Loved One, going through traumatic life stressors can be as invasive as being thrown in a foxhole and fired at. We do need to praise God when we can walk away alive, but we also shouldn't bury the pain of it. We shouldn't linger on it, but we should acknowledge and deal with it so we can properly heal and move on.

One of the things my dad taught me was the value of human emotion. When I was in college, I had a bad break up with my first serious boyfriend. Dad took his tear-flowing daughter to Mary's Restaurant for one of those turtle sundaes that I couldn't eat, but just sat and played with.

"Babes," he said, "I know you aren't going to want to hear this now and I'm sure you won't appreciate this until much later, but rejoice in what you are experiencing right now. God gave us an array of human emotion and you are privileged enough to be experiencing one that not everyone will. I know it hurts and I wish I could help you with that, but it will make you stronger. That day you finally wake up and realize the rock in your stomach is gone, you will feel like a person who's made it through the fire and your perspective of life will change forever. You will have one more complicated piece of you for someone to understand and love someday… the right someone." At the time I wanted to tell him where to cram his strawberry sundae, but I listened because he had never steered me wrong.

This is never an easy message to receive, but sometimes we need to celebrate the difficult things we go through. God is allowing us experiences that may sometimes be painful but, in the end, grow and shape us, and make us healthier.

My physical heart felt stronger, but I still had a lot of work to do on my emotional heart. God was right. My heart issues were the starting point all those years ago for feeling rejected and alone. It made me feel different. I hated that word so much. After my heart surgery, God said something unexpected.

"You *are* different. Because I *made* you different."

For a time, these words magically changed my perspective, but they didn't take root. *Different* was still a bad word in my vocabulary, and it would be a while before I acquired a new dictionary.

Just like the doctors who brought me back into the surgery center to re-test what they had fixed, don't be surprised if you find yourself in a situation similar to the one that initially broke you. God may very well be re-testing your heart to ensure everything is holding. Which is exactly what happened with me.

For now, I still had the blindfold on, and I was about to go back into traffic. Walking backward.

Caroline Klug

Chapter 11
Arid Places

I've always been rather risk averse. I steer pretty clear of things like water skiing, downhill skiing, bungee jumping, and skydiving. Pretty much anything that could separate an appendage. *I rather like my limbs attached.* There was one time when Jim was trying to get me to use his stand-up jet ski, and I'm pretty sure an "oo oo wait wait" came out. For those of you with an astute memory, that's an extra "wait" thrown in there. I didn't bother mentioning that configuration in the prior chapter, because it's reserved only for rare, category five threats. Besides that time, I typically aim for safety and comfort. I wish I could say the same about the train wreck of personal decisions that followed my heart surgery.

> "When an impure spirit comes out of a person, it goes through arid places seeking rest and does not find it. Then it says, 'I will return to the house I left.' When it arrives, it finds the house unoccupied, swept clean and put in order. Then it goes and takes with it seven other spirits more wicked than itself, and they go in and live

there. And the final condition of that person is worse than the first. That is how it will be with this wicked generation." Matthew 12:43-45

Before we look inside the wrecked train cars, we need to back up to when the train was sitting at the station, ready to take off, so we can see what caused the accident.

***

Life was good. My physical heart was strong again, and I was well on the way to emotional healing. My faith had never been stronger and, little by little, I found myself doing more and more for God.

Writing has been a passion of mine since I was in my early twenties. Only, at the time, I thought I was going to write popular business books like *Who Moved My Cheese?* I had my dreams and, although the spirit of them were right, they didn't completely align with God's yet. I was sitting on my living room couch when God interrupted my dream with a sentence, penetrating every part of my being.

"I want you to write books for *Me*."

It was so clear and unmistakable that I didn't have time or reason to dismiss it. Instead, I did what most good human beings would do, and I panicked. I panicked because I didn't know a thing about writing Christian books. My immediate response to God was that He was asking the wrong person, because all I'd do is regurgitate whatever I had read in some other Christian authors' books. Then He did it again. That same bold and beautiful, inaudible voice, spoke just as clearly.

"Ask Me for insights."

I can't explain the way I felt, other than to say my spirit was quickened to listen, like I needed to take this as seriously as the air I breathe. That very day, I went to the store and bought a notebook. God not only interrupted my dream, but He disrupted my daily quiet time too. Up until that point, I had made it a practice to open my Bible and read a few paragraphs, or maybe a whole chapter, close the Bible, and check the box for the day. What began happening next set a new course and a new fire that would change the way I saw everything.

Each morning, before opening my Bible (remember, this was before smartphones and Bible apps), I would rest my hands on it, close my eyes, and ask God to inspire me with His insights. I asked Him to show me things I might otherwise miss. I also asked Him to give me spiritual wisdom to understand what I was reading. What happened next was nothing short of revolutionary for me.

> "Ask and it will be given to you; seek and you will find; knock and the door will be opened to you. For everyone who asks receives; the one who seeks finds; and to the one who knocks, the door will be opened." Matthew 7:7-8

You can't fool God. He knows what runs through every fiber of your heart and mind. And that includes sincerity, which is what happened to be running through mine. I don't

Caroline Klug

know how to describe it other than to tell you I came with an expectant heart. I *expected* to hear something from Him, and you know what? I *did*. I've never done drugs, but I bet the euphoria I felt hearing His voice, having my eyes see something new, or gaining some understanding I didn't have before, was better than any high a person could manufacture. He was *real*. He was *alive*. His *Word* was alive. It was *just* like it said in the Bible. My relationship with God quickly went from head to heart, and it was transforming me.

I started writing down some of these insights. I was so excited about what God was saying, I shared them with a few of my friends from church. They told me I should start a blog.

What's a blog?

I had no idea. I had never even heard the word before. Fast forward about six months, and I had a website where I posted these insights and the little stories they turned into.

Something weird happened. People started signing up to be alerted when I had a new blog out there. *What? Who are you and why do you care? Where is Namibia?* I know that's the whole point of the blog, but I guess I never thought anyone other than my family and friends would sign up. Especially people from countries whose names I couldn't pronounce correctly.

Then something weirder happened. People started coming to me. At work. At church. At home. They wanted to *talk*. They would share their troubles and ask for advice and prayer. It got so frequent, I actually had to start coming into work an hour earlier, just to make sure I got my work done.

In short order, I found myself leading a Bible study at work. I didn't really know at the time that there were a lot of pre-written studies out there, so I made up my own. We had a faithful few who would gather every week, but with prayer and more prayer, our little group went from five to forty in a matter of a few months.

Then, the senior pastor at the Christian church I attended asked if I would consider leading their Women's Ministry. I was honored, but terrified. That was more than two hundred women. But there was something stirring in my heart and I knew it was the right place for me. So I said yes, and began facilitating and teaching weekly studies to them too.

I started getting requests to come and speak at women's gatherings and retreats. Although I was typically pretty comfortable in front of people, this seemed like a whole different plate of pasta. One I thought I might throw up. I was scared, and I felt a lot of responsibility. These women were *paying* to be here, and *expecting* to get something useful from me. God led me through it, but I had to learn it wasn't about me. It was just about being faithful to receive and deliver the message, by His grace, and leave the rest up to Him.

As if that wasn't amazing enough, shortly after that I started holding weekend women's retreats under the nonprofit I had created, KingdomGlory Ministries. *And women showed up.* So many came that the beautiful lake home we were using had to be supplemented by the hotel down the road. I couldn't believe it.

While all this was going on, I was still a single mom and had a demanding job. I continued to blog every week, but never seriously thought about writing a book yet. You see, I had a humble prayer in my heart that went something like this:

"Lord, if it's possible, I'd really like to wait to publish a real book until I'm with my forever husband – the one You bless me with – so my last name on my books never changes."

I know that sounds shallow, but it came from a place of simple sincerity. Coupled, of course, with the notion that God would be delivering my forever husband *soon*. I mean, why wouldn't He? I was doing *everything* He asked of me. I was pouring my life and heart into ministry for Him. Of course it was *His* turn to reward me for that.

But that forever husband wasn't delivered on time. *My* idea of time. Time went on, and I continued to minister. I continued to grieve through my desires while I watched all the people around me get what they wanted. People who weren't serving God the way *I* was serving Him. It felt like a raw deal to me, and my heart began to harden. Bitterness and Resentment both showed up at my front door. With suitcases. And I let them both in. Have you ever tried living with two very noisy people? No matter what room of your house you go in, you can't seem to escape their voices.

> *I can't minister effectively without a real partner to share this with.*
>
> *Everyone else is doing whatever they want. Why can't I do what I want?*
>
> *I have too much on my plate and no time for myself.*
>
> *I'm doing everything for God and He's doing nothing for me.*
>
> *I'm never going to be happy without a husband.*

Tell Them

These are the lies straight from hell that permeated my mind. Those two voices wreaked a lot of havoc, and weakened my already fragile being. Speaking of hell, I might need to dig that deep to get to these next bones. Here goes. Make sure you tether yourself to something while we work our way down.

While I was leading Women's Ministry, that particular church had a guideline that asked their ministry leaders to abstain from alcohol. I loved wine, but it seemed an easy thing to give up in return for being able to do what I felt called to do. I did that faithfully for the two years I held that position. Until that one night I didn't.

I had to go on a work trip, so Bitterness, Resentment, and I all packed up our bags and traveled to our destination. There were two guys going as well, one of whom would often flirt with me at the office. He was someone all the ladies thought was handsome, and they wanted his attention. One time at work, I heard someone in the next cubical call him, talk for a moment, and then hang up. He told her he was busy and couldn't talk right now. Seconds later my phone rang. It was him. He was calling for no reason, just to say hi. Normally that might be flattering, but he was married. That was a closed door. Up to that point, I was polite but not enabling.

That evening, we all went to dinner. He sat next to me in the booth, so I was squished between him and Temptation, and Temptation wouldn't stop pushing me. The waitress showed up to take our drink orders, and asked me what I wanted. I knew the words. *Nothing for me, thanks. Water is fine.* Before I could say anything, Resentment ordered me a mixed drink. What was I supposed to do? Turn it down? That would have been rude, so I drank it, along with the next several drinks Bitterness followed that up with.

I never have more than two drinks in an evening. I'm a light weight, and anything more than that would leave me intoxicated. *I already failed. Having another won't matter.* Given the fact I had not had a drop of alcohol for the last two years, I'm wagering those same two drinks would have had even more impact on me. Only, I didn't have two drinks. I had four.

Dear One, we all fall on our face. But just because you fall doesn't mean what you do next doesn't matter. That's like saying eating an entire chocolate cake doesn't matter because I've already eaten a burger. Every calorie adds up. Every action matters, and it's never too late to pull it back in and do the right thing.

It was the lie that nothing else mattered after I had that drink that poisoned me. It was also the culmination of my hardened heart saying enough. I wanted to do what I wanted to do. To heck with the consequences. Unfortunately, it's really hard to access consequences when you're stumbling drunk.

2007 was a rough year for pop singer, Britney Spears. She used her umbrella to beat the snot out of a photographer's car a few days after she shaved all the hair off her head. One could say she hit social rock bottom during that time. There was a popular meme going around that said, *"If Britney Spears can make it through 2007, then I can make it through today."* If, for some reason, you're having difficulty recalling who this is, you might better recognize her from her popular song, "Oops!... I Did it Again," which could also be the title of this chapter.

Go ahead and let your imaginations roll. I barely remember the rest of that night, but I know I slept with him. Oddly enough, there was one other piece of my memory that felt very clear to me. It was when I was standing with him at the entrance to my hotel, with my hand on the long, vertical silver door handle. That memory haunted me for years after, because my only explanation was that I was being given a merciful opportunity to shut down whatever foul ball was about to be hit. I had an opportunity – a moment of clarity – to do the right thing. But I didn't.

The next morning was nothing short of a nightmare for me. I was reeling, and couldn't believe the size of the cliff I had fallen off. The worst part is that I had a meeting with him that morning. I shook through that whole meeting, but neither of us said a word about it. I can tell you, of all my indiscretions, I had never felt so disgusted with myself than I did in that moment, unable to take it back, and unsure how to move forward.

I made God a promise when I first started teaching Bible studies. In my early but hungry heart, I desired for my words to be anointed by Him, and I promised Him if I were ever not right with Him, I would not step foot in front of people and try to minister. I was now staring that promise in the face and I had to follow through. I quit. Everything. I stepped down from Women's Ministry. I got a replacement for the work Bible Study. I stopped blogging. People felt my shut down and they stopped coming to me. Everything. Just. Stopped.

Anger was an easier emotion to deal with than hurt, so I stayed angry. I did a lot of feeling sorry for myself. I felt like so many things had been taken from me, and it wasn't fair. I let the old cassette tapes roll, and even started recording a few new ones of my own.

> *Because I did what I did, there's no way I can ever go back to ministry.*
>
> *Because I can never go back to ministry, I don't need to adhere to higher standards.*
>
> *Because I don't need to adhere to higher standards, I can do what I want.*

That's exactly what I did. I drank. I flirted with men, whether they were single or not. I dated. A lot. Thankfully, I didn't sleep around, but my dating choices were not made with a lot of long-term ambition in mind. My spirit was like the arid place in Matthew 12. I had swept it clean but a whole new batch of bad moved in. That whole time was like a dangerous and irritating game of spiritual Whac-a-Mole. I even had an unhealthy crush on my psychiatrist. Facepalm.

When you're hungry for love and acceptance, even the most basic of kindness can be misinterpreted, because you're seeing what you want to see. You're seeing what you *need* to see.

Soon after that, I entered into a relationship with a man who was separated from his wife. Not divorced. Separated. They had been separated for years, but their divorce was pending for financially beneficial reasons. It caught me very much by surprise, as it did him, but at the time it seemed like a pleasant one. We seemed to genuinely care for one another, and it was good. By anyone's basic standards, he was a good guy. He wasn't a Christian, but he was decent and kind, which is just what I thought I needed. I was with him for a few years. He lived out of state, so we only saw each other a few times per month, but I had real feelings, and wanted to see it work.

Satan wasn't surprised. Satan knew what I had been feeling – I had been wearing it openly on my face for months. Putting this person in my path was no accident. It was another temptation. One I failed. And I felt the consequence of it. Because of his separation, we had to hide our relationship for a long time, and there was always an undercurrent of fear and guilt because of that.

Cherished One, whenever you find yourself in the middle of something you think you need to hide, that should be an immediate danger sign that what you are about to do isn't of God. Nothing that is of God needs to be hidden. Only things of Satan need to live in the dark.

I thought I would be happier when his divorce was finalized. I wasn't. Even though I didn't have the guilt of his separation any more, there was still something missing. A void. A dark hole to an even darker abyss. I didn't feel whole, and I knew why. I was still trying to fill a supernatural hole with natural material. I was trying to put sugar water into the gas tank of a BMW. Not only would it not work, but it would eventually destroy the engine.

The Type A in me knew I had to do something, so I did something I had not done in a very long time. I got on my knees, and I prayed for wisdom. I even cited the Scripture in James 1 where it says anyone who asks can get wisdom, no matter what their standing. *As if I had to remind God of His own rules.* Then I got brave and had a serious discussion with that man about where God was or could be in our relationship. He told me he was very supportive of my faith and beliefs, but it just wasn't for him.

Tangent. During my second marriage, I did my first forty-day fast, eating only fruits and vegetables. By day twenty-one, I remember vowing to never eat another piece of broccoli. Broccoli and I have made up since then, but it was an extremely tough thing for me to do. During one of my especially trying days, I had to go to the grocery store. I was feeling very weak, temptation wise, and recall sitting in my car and praying for God to give me the strength to walk through that store without buying something outside of my fast and failing. Things were going well, and I began to get nervous as I approached where they were baking the rotisserie chicken. I had to walk past it in order to get to what I needed. It wasn't until it was behind me that I realized something odd. I couldn't smell anything. I thought it was so strange, that I backed up a few steps, within range of the chicken. Still nothing. My heart skipped a beat and I pushed my cart forward a few aisles and turned down *the* aisle. The coffee aisle. Nothing. I couldn't smell anything. I will never forget it, and it will always be embedded in my mind as a supernatural answer to prayer.

Back to "Jesus just isn't for me." Because we were long distance, we were having this conversation over the phone. What happened over the next few minutes I can only akin to not smelling coffee in the grocery store. I allowed an awkward silence to build before I found these words leaving my mouth:

"That would be like me telling you I really support how you feel about your kids and you spending time with them, but I don't want to spend time with them. It's just not my thing."

That man not wanting to share Jesus with me felt as ridiculous as that statement I had just made. It was a moment of clarity which gave me the courage to end that relationship.

"Let me get this straight. You're breaking up with me because I don't love Jesus?"

"Yes."

That was it. That was the end. There was no long, drawn out conversation after. Only a few apologies and the click of the call ending. The strangest part was, I wasn't upset. I knew I should be. I had been *in love* with the man. I should have been bawling my eyes out and putting down a half gallon of chocolate almond fudge ice cream. But I just wasn't. I couldn't smell the coffee. I tried to smell it. I even tried to imagine what it would taste like, but there was nothing.

> "Do not be anxious about anything, but in every situation, by prayer and petition, with thanksgiving, present your requests to God. And the peace of God, which transcends all understanding, will guard your hearts and your minds in Christ Jesus."
> Philippians 4:6-7

How elated God must be when we stand up and fight for Him. And how merciful He is to help us in that fight, in so many unexpected ways. I had every reason to celebrate and run back home to my Father like the prodigal child, but one act of bravery doesn't always mean you're healed. I was still alone, and looking for love in all the wrong places. Which is the mindset that lead me into the last and final affair I had – the one I talked about in the chapter, Hell on Earth. But I left you hanging. I didn't tell you what happened with that affair. Now that we're through what was in between the book ends, I'd like to finish that story, and tell you how real love found *me*.

> "Then Jesus told them this parable: 'Suppose one of you has a hundred sheep and loses one of them. Doesn't he leave the ninety-nine in the open country and go after the lost sheep until he finds it?'" Luke 15:3-4

Chapter 12
Leaving the 99

It was, hands down, the most difficult feedback I had ever received. I didn't want to accept it, let alone believe it. I wanted God to be talking about someone else. Anyone else but me. The truth of His words penetrated my heart, and the shock of it ushered me into a long silence.

> "Wisdom will save you also from the adulterous woman, from the wayward woman with her seductive words .... Surely her house leads down to death and her paths to the spirits of the dead. None who go to her return or attain the paths of life." Proverbs 2:16,18-19

The extramarital affair I went into detail on was my final act of sinful freefalling. It was the culmination of a reality I had a hard time facing. But facing it changed *everything*.

I *was* that wayward woman. The woman in Proverbs 2.

One could argue those men were the wayward ones, but I need to own my role in all of that. I should have known better. I *did* know better, but in my search for acceptance, I had knowingly led other men down the path of death. That is a hard reality to face. It's shameful and embarrassing to say that out loud and call it what it is. But sometimes that's exactly what we need to do to bring us to a point where we can see and hear more clearly.

Once I was finally able to acknowledge that, rather than allow God's conviction to empower positive change, I allowed Satan to condemn me. I experienced a grave amount of shame. Hence, the dirt-digging, bone-burying party. I held onto that shame for a long time. It was just as God had told me. I was forgiven, but I wasn't free. I was chained to the shame of my past, and those shackles continued to dig deeper into my already tender and wounded flesh.

When you hide or lie about things, that causes an extreme amount of duress. Hiding things about myself made me feel guilty, and carrying around that guilt wore me down and eroded me from the inside out.

There was a show that used to be on television called, *The Biggest Loser*, in which contestants who were excessively overweight worked with well-known fitness trainers for several months to lose the weight and get in shape. At a certain point toward the end of each season, there would be an episode where contestants had to walk and hike a course with the weight they had lost strapped to them. As they got closer and closer to the finish, they got to remove more and more of the weight, until they were able to cross the finish line with no extra weight on them.

Burdened One, carrying weight you were never meant to carry can cause a lot of damage, physically, mentally, and spiritually. That weight stresses your body and joints, making it difficult to move forward. It crushes your spirit, flooding

Tell Them

you with oppressive and depressive feelings. It lies to you, telling you that you're unlovable and unworthy to come before God.

This is how I felt in every sense. I'm guessing this might be how you feel if there's something you're hiding or feeling shame from. You might feel all of that weight is on you, and you can't take another step. If so, then you need to hear the next part of my love story. Because it's yours too.

> "Then Jesus told them this parable: 'Suppose one of you has a hundred sheep and loses one of them. Doesn't he leave the ninety-nine in the open country and go after the lost sheep until he finds it? And when he finds it, he joyfully puts it on his shoulders and goes home. Then he calls his friends and neighbors together and says, 'Rejoice with me; I have found my lost sheep.' I tell you that in the same way there will be more rejoicing in heaven over one sinner who repents than over ninety-nine righteous persons who do not need to repent.'" Luke 15:3-7

Even in the darkest parts of my sin, I heard God mercifully calling out to me. The weight of my sin held me down and I couldn't move. It crushed my spirit and convinced me I was unworthy. Jesus knew I was lost. He left the ninety-nine other sheep and He searched for me. Even writing that still makes me cry. He was searching for *me*. After what I had done.

Guys.

Are you hearing this? I hope so, because it's huge. Don't ever let anyone mislead you that God isn't loving. Don't ever let anyone convince you that the things you've done put a permanent barrier between you and Him.

Don't ever believe the lie that you can't come back.

You could be in the deepest, darkest, dirtiest, and most dreadful hole there is, and your loving Father will find you. He will leave the ninety-nine and He will find *you*. Not only will He find you, but He'll jump down in the hole with you, pick you up, and carry you out. All you need to do is ask. And that's what I finally did.

Amidst my gut-wrenching turmoil and confusion, I got on my knees and I cried out. That doesn't mean I repented of my sin and came asking for forgiveness. It means even though every part of my fleshly and selfish heart wanted what it wanted, there was something louder crying out from the deepest recesses of my soul. I was His. I would *always* be His. My heart loved Him and knew there was nothing on this earth that would satisfy my heart like He can. I was so tired and hurt and exhausted. I knew I couldn't live like that anymore. I couldn't keep running. Like an addict fighting an addiction, knowing better but feeling utterly incapable of fighting it, I fell to my knees and cried out to the only One I knew could save me.

In hindsight, I'm confident God saw the sincerity of my heart in that moment. I sobbed as I told Him I didn't want to be apart from Him anymore, but I didn't have the strength to let go of the sinful relationship I was in. I needed Him to help. I needed Him to do what I couldn't.

Words cannot describe how difficult that prayer was for me. I knew what it meant. I knew it meant more earthly loss for me. More grieving than I thought I could bear. But I had

Tell Them

finally gotten to the point where the pain I was feeling from both the separation from God and the situation I was in outweighed whatever bit of happiness that sin brought me. I was so tired. Exhausted. In pain. I was face-down, my tears, mascara, and snot all mixing with the carpet beneath me. That moment was really messy. Beautifully messy, because I had finally surrendered.

Within days of that prayer, the man I was having an affair with walked away. I wish I could tell you the obedience of crying out for help brought relief and joy, but not right away. I was shocked, even though I shouldn't have been, and I was devastated. In my mind, I had lost something, and I was grieving. There was some relief over the lie being over, but it was still very painful. I could smell the coffee. I tell you this because I don't want to sugarcoat reality. The reality is, doing the right thing doesn't always feel good. But the other side of that reality is, it won't *always* feel that way.

> "When He had said this, Jesus called in a loud voice, 'Lazarus, come out!' The dead man came out, his hands and feet wrapped with strips of linen, and a cloth around his face. Jesus said to them, 'Take off the grave clothes and let him go.'" John 11:43-44

I was dead. In the grave. My grave clothes bound me as tightly as the sin that consumed me. But Jesus cried out. He came to the tomb I was in and He called me out. He made me alive again. I was dead, and then I wasn't. In this scene with Lazarus, when Jesus told them to take off his grave clothes and let him go, He was talking to the people who were there mourning his death. For me, I hear something a little different. I hear Jesus telling Satan to take off my grave clothes and let me go. Jesus left the ninety-nine and He found me. He heard my cry and He found me. He didn't yell, He didn't shame, and He didn't condemn. He simply loved me, and He was merciful enough to answer my cry for help.

I spent a long time regretting that I wasn't the one who walked away. Not because of spite or anything petty, but simply out of a desire to walk out my obedience. Through years of healing, Jesus showed me what *He* saw, and it will forever tender my heart.

> "'Do not be afraid, you worm Jacob, little Israel, do not fear, for I Myself will help you,' declares the Lord, your Redeemer, the Holy One of Israel." Isaiah 41:14

I *did* walk out my obedience. I *did* honor His cry out to me with a cry back of my own. It may not have been in the form of a break-up, but in the form of the surrender that happened in my heart when I slid onto my knees and begged Him to do what I couldn't. I knew it would be painful, but I wanted Jesus more than I wanted anything or anyone else, and I just needed help to get healthy. God honors the sincerity of our hearts.

Although I made it out of that mess, it took a lot for me to get past the lie that I couldn't minister to people after what I had done. Which is kind of a selfish thought, if you think about it. Once again, I was making it about me. I was deciding *for* God what He was and wasn't allowed to do with my past. I was defining the boundaries of His forgiveness, and limiting the scope of His power and authority. I was burying things which could and should be used for the building of His Kingdom.

In reality, belief in the lie that I couldn't come back meant I was choosing *not* to believe in the validity of the many incredible heart and life transformations in both the Old and New Testaments. God called countless people out of their figurative graves for things that would be, by today's standards, shocking. If you think the Bible is all about love and butterflies, think again. It happens to be filled with scandal. And forgiveness.

A most incredible reminder of this is our own King David. David was a shepherd boy, and the youngest of eight brothers. David loved God, and spent his days faithfully guarding the flock. During this time, the Israelites were facing off against the Philistine army. The Bible tells us that twice per day, morning and night, for forty days, the giant of the Philistine army would come out, in between the army lines, and challenge the Israelites to send one person of their choosing to fight him, and decide the fate of the war with a single one-on-one combat (1 Samuel 17). It says the Israelites, *including their King, Saul*, were terrified. Even the king was terrified!

What nine-foot giant are you facing, which simply looks too large to defeat? What terrifies you?

Little David was sent to the army lines, not to fight, but to bring his older brothers some food. While he was there, he witnessed Goliath's rant in the valley. Not only did he hear the challenge to fight, but he heard Goliath taunting and mocking the God he loved. It was game on. David volunteered to fight the giant.

Caroline Klug

What would you do to stand up for God? He certainly doesn't need us to defend His honor, but... would you?

To make a long story short, with a slingshot and a stone, this runt of the litter took down the giant the whole of the Israeli army feared and, through a course of events, gained favor with the Israelites and eventually succeeded King Saul and was anointed King. David was King, he loved God, and all was well. Until that one day it wasn't.

David was out one evening when he saw Bathsheba for the first time. She was beautiful. And naked. At least I assume she was, because it says she was bathing when he saw her from his rooftop. He was on his roof at night, looking down on someone who thought they had privacy. Indulging in the view rather than walking away was his first mistake. I'm guessing the images he allowed in played in his mind until curiosity and compromise got the best of him. That's when he sent someone to find her and bring her to him. This *married* woman, whose husband was away fighting in David's army.

We get very little from the next few sentences that say, "She came to him, and he slept with her" (2 Samuel 11:4). This next part is taking interpretational liberty, but I'm guessing he took what he wanted. And even if it wasn't by force, it might have been by intimidation. In those times, it would have been incredibly intimidating to be called into the King's chambers. Saying no was likely akin to asking for death. But just for giggles, let's go one step farther and assume she slept with him of her own free will. He made the offer and maybe she thought it was exciting to be seduced by the king. Either way, David sinned gravely, and brought

Tell Them

her down with him. The Lord was displeased (2 Samuel 11:27).

The scandal doesn't stop there. It gets worse. And worse. And then, just a little bit worse.

She sends word to David that she's pregnant. One of the worst aspects of being caught up in sin is trying to use *more* sin to cover it up – which is exactly what David did. He called Bathsheba's husband home from the war and tried to entice him to spend the night at home and knock boots with his wife. Problem solved, right? Not exactly. You see, her husband had too much integrity to engage in such pleasures while his men were suffering at war, so he refused to go home. Instead, he slept at the palace entrance. Manipulation and deceit didn't work for David, so in his panic, he upped the ante and turned to murder. David had Bathsheba's husband sent to the front lines, where the fighting was the worst. But he didn't stop there. He gave orders for the others around him to withdraw once there, to make sure he would be struck down.

Her husband was killed, and Bathsheba was brought to David's palace to live, where she had their baby. This is the point when Jerry Springer called, to book David on his show. But thankfully, David declined, because this story didn't just end in death and destruction. It ended in forgiveness and redemption. Yes, David did try to hide his piles of sin, but he was eventually exposed, fessed up, and received God's forgiveness. We are still being blessed today by his many beautiful and heart-felt psalms.

How happy must it make God when we own up to our decisions and lay them at His feet? Sweet One, God is no fool. He already knows what you did, so the simple act of acknowledging and showing God the respect He deserves goes a long way. When we can step out of our sin and be alive with Him, I have to believe He is pleased with us, and there is much to celebrate. We get to take off our grave clothes and put on our banquet attire. *Pass the beef tips, please.*

I wish I could end the story there. God did forgive David, but we still need to talk about the consequences. The first was that God denied David the building of the temple he dreamed of. Instead, this temple was built by his son, Solomon. However disappointing that may have been, there was one consequence much more heartbreaking. You could say it was a grave consequence. Literally. The price he paid for his actions? The death of his child. I find myself holding my breath when I read that, so incredibly thankful God spared my own. I am venturing outside my education when I say this, but I can't help but wonder if David's literal consequence was a warning shot for us, of the negative impacts our kids could face as a result of not having a parent who is walking in truth. It might not be their literal death, but it could mean their spiritual death. Again, this is just a point of speculation for me.

I wanted to go into detail on David's story because I want you to see something important. God called David "a man after His own heart" (1 Samuel 13:14). *After His own heart.* I can't think of a better compliment to receive from the King of kings. From the God of love who *is* love. From the heart God Himself. And God spoke this of a man who did such unspeakable things. I have to believe David was ashamed, and had to spend a fair amount of time healing from all of this. But did he ever imagine that His love story would go on to be a source of light for billions of other people across so many generations?

Tell Them

"But everything exposed by the light becomes visible – and everything that is illuminated becomes a light." Ephesians 5:13

My heart raced when I saw this passage for the first time. I have read the book of Ephesians more times than I can count, but I had not *seen* this passage before. God had put the pieces of my broken heart back together, and this passage was the hope I needed to bring my heart to *you* and tell my story.

Forgiven One, Satan wants you to think the pieces of your story are sharp, jagged, and meant to cut. What God is showing us in this beautiful passage is that the pieces of your story are there to reflect the love of Christ and illuminate a path for others to find healing and redemption. God doesn't say *some* things illuminated will become light. He says *everything.*

When I read the account of Lazarus, I like to envision something beyond Lazarus having his grave clothes taken off. I like to imagine what must have been an incredibly joyful reunion. For four days his family thought he was dead and gone, never to return this side of heaven. Then, he wasn't. He was standing right in front of them. In front of all the people who loved him. In front of Jesus.

When you repent of sin, heal from sin, and walk in the light, Jesus and all of heaven rejoices. But that's not all. Every person along your path who ever prayed for you, loved you, and counseled you are standing around that tomb you are no longer in. Whether it's people in your past or present, they are rejoicing with you.

For me, that list of people standing outside my tomb is long. There are countless people who prayed for me and supported me. Included on that list is my dad. Even though he has passed away, I believe all the prayers he sent up for me are still being honored today. *Thanks, Dad. You were a wonderful example to me of how to love and pray for my own daughter.*

The love of God never ceases to amaze me. Its power and fortitude can bring the dead back to life. When I was in spiritual hospice, my hope was gone, and I had resigned myself to my impending death.

But God.

I love those two words so much. He heard me crying out in pain. He left the ninety-nine and He came for me. He'll come for you, too. He'll meet you wherever you are. The depth doesn't matter.

> "Therefore, if anyone is in Christ, the new creation has come: the old has gone, the new is here!"
> 2 Corinthians 5:17

When God calls you out, you need to leave that cancer in the grave where it belongs. It's easy to want to bring it with you, but that won't heal you. It will only be something Satan uses to distract you and keep you from the light. Distraction is dangerous, because it takes us off the path. And Satan doesn't fight fair. His army is made up of serial killers.

Let's go meet a few of them.

Chapter 13
Serial Killers

I'll never forget watching book sales come in after *Stolen* launched. I didn't really know what to expect, but based on comments from other authors in my writing groups, it seemed to be doing great. The sales I had received in the first few weeks were more than some of the other self-published authors said they had seen their first *year*. I was feeling so good, I decided to waste a few minutes of my life scrolling through my Facebook news feed. That's when I saw it.

Another author I'm connected to put a post out saying how thrilled she was that her new book sold so many copies in the first two days. Her number was *three times* what I had after two weeks. Only hers was from two days. And she had one of those nauseating little excited faces to indicate how she was feeling. All my good vibes flatlined. I wanted to gouge the little stars right out of her emoticon's eyes. Meet our first serial killer, Comparison.

Comparison is the teenage girl who seems to have all the most popular material possessions you could never afford. She tells you what you have isn't enough, and talks you into shoplifting so you can have them too. She tells you that you *deserve* those things. And when you get caught, she's nowhere to be found as you're hauled off in cuffs, wondering what method of murder your parents are going to use on you.

When we let her hang out with us, we're assuming we know all the pieces and parts of someone's story, and how it's going to end. We also assume all the elements of our situations are the same. What if this woman spent three times as much on marketing than I did? What if this was her fifth book? What if she had her book on pre-order three times longer than I did? In that moment, none of those questions registered in my brain. All I saw were the numbers, and that made my eyeballs green with jealousy.

The truth is, that woman earned those sales. Whether it was through her diligence in marketing, discipline in producing multiple books and gaining a following, or simply because she put out a fantastic product that people wanted, she did the work and earned the reward. A better response from me would have been to appreciate her success and seek to understand how I could learn from it, so I could do better next time. Instead, I allowed Satan to drop Comparison off for a sleepover, and we painted our nails with unhealthy thoughts and feelings. Those feelings took my focus off celebrating the orders I did have, and made me feel as though it wasn't enough. Which translated to me feeling *I* wasn't enough.

Comparing yourself to others can lead you to feelings of inadequacy, which is victim thinking. I didn't sell less books because I'm less of a human being. I sold less books because I didn't do as much as she did. If you want what someone else has, try doing what they did. *Just sayin'.*

There's another touchy element to this that takes a lot of maturity to process and accept. It's entirely possible this woman sold more books because her book was better. *Ouch.* Which leads us to the next killer on the list.

This one suffers from multiple personality disorder. Sometimes Pride is an arrogant S.O.B. who lures us into egotistical thinking. He puts people down; it's his way of building himself up. Pride fears no one will naturally lift him up, so he pushes others down and creates the illusion of being better than they are. And when it appears someone has something he doesn't, he can't be happy for them. Instead, he's jealous.

Not all feelings of pride are bad. It's okay to feel good about something you've accomplished. It's okay to get excited about a big win or a long-worked-for goal or dream being realized. What's not okay, is when Pride tells you to hold yourself higher than someone else because of those victories. When he convinces you that someone else's failure is merely a mirror to your success, that's a problem.

> "For by the grace given to me I say to everyone among you not to think of himself more highly than he ought to think, but to think with sober judgment, each according to the measure of faith that God has assigned." Romans 12:3

Other times, Pride won't interact with anyone. He refuses to let others in, and never asks for help, even if he's experiencing a life-threatening situation. Usually that's because he's embarrassed or even ashamed. It's a no-brainer for us to call an ambulance when we fear our life is in danger.

Caroline Klug

Why is it so hard for us to call on God and other Christians when our spiritual life is just as much at risk?

Jim and I are currently preparing for sail-cation. That's our term for when we spend our vacation on the sailboat. We are planning to sail across Lake Michigan for the first time, which is no joke. It takes over twelve hours to cross, in perfect conditions, and is a very ocean-like body of fresh water.

Jim put me in charge of testing the distress button inside our sailboat before we leave. It's part of the VHF radio, and is pre-programmed to send information about us and our boat and location to the U.S. Coast Guard, as well as any neighboring vessels within a ten to thirty-mile radius. It also supplies emergency contact information. God forbid, if something goes wrong, it will be critical to alert help as quickly and efficiently as possible.

When something life-threatening is happening, minutes matter, and those minutes can be the difference between life and death. Communicating all that information quickly with the touch of a button allows us to keep focus on whatever we need to do to address the threat, like bailing water from our boat to keep afloat. Because I'm in charge of the distress button, I will be sure to keep an astute focus on things. There might be some questionable situations that arise, which will require a hard call. For example, if a two-hundred-pound sturgeon starts swimming around our boat, I might be like, "Oo oo wait... do I push the button, er no?" (If you live in the Midwest, then you know "er" is an acceptable substitute for "or"). Of course, it might be embarrassing to explain my rationale to the Coast Guard when they show up, but I take my responsibilities very seriously, and will risk the embarrassment in order to save

Tell Them

our lives from what I will only assume is pending death by a shark-sized fish. This leads us into the introduction of our next killer, because we can't allow him to get in the way when our lives depend on it.

This killer is as notorious as Richard "The Iceman" Kuklinski. He earned his nickname because he liked to freeze the bodies of his victims to confuse the police on time of death. The Iceman may have died in prison in 2006, but his mentor is still alive and active today, and goes by the name of Shame.

Shame is a General in Satan's army, and is ordered to weaken and debilitate people until it eventually kills them. Like The Iceman, he tends to leave people confused about their real time of death. It's not the sin or trauma that kills someone, but the lie they tell to hide the sin or trauma.

I'm convinced one of the deadliest weapons Satan uses against us is getting us to believe the truth will hurt us more than the lie. There is so much power in hiding and concealing things, and it's not good power. It's the kind of thing that rots your bones and significantly reduces your quality of life – both physically and spiritually. With every rotten bone we bury, we give control over to the enemy.

It can be terrifying to tell the truth, especially when we are the ones in the wrong, and we're afraid of what others might think of us because of what we did. Loved One, do not be manipulated and debilitated by the enemy. Remember what we said in the beginning?

No lie can overcome the truth, but the truth can overcome any lie.

Caroline Klug

Let's dive into the profile of a serial killer that has left more bodies in the woods than there are Chick-fil-A nuggets in Utah. Standing seven feet and four inches tall and weighing in at five hundred pounds is not just the once-living professional French wrestler, Andre the Giant, but one of our most prolific serial killers, Doubt.

Doubt has the ability to step into the ring and body slam you before the beginning bell even sounds off. He's not gentlemanly, and he certainly doesn't follow the rules of the ring. He's rude and takes advantage of any moment you might have your guard down. And once he sits on you, it's awfully hard to get up.

> "If any of you lacks wisdom, you should ask God, who gives generously to all without finding fault, and it will be given to you. But when you ask, you must believe and not doubt, because the one who doubts is like a wave of the sea, blown and tossed by the wind. That person should not expect to receive anything from the Lord. Such a person is double-minded and unstable in all they do." James 1:5-8

When you let Doubt in the ring with you, it's game over. If you see him coming, refuse to engage. I've made a lot of critical errors in life by thinking I could handle or manage my feelings of doubt. I think about the relationship I had with my dad, and all the ways he loved and invested in me. There was a lot I should have gleaned from that example – so many parallels to my relationship with God. My dad gave me every reason to trust him. He always made it abundantly clear he was in my corner. So has God. But sometimes, we don't trust what we know of our heavenly

Tell Them

Father. Instead, we pick a fight with Doubt. In most cases, Doubt doesn't come to the fight alone. He brings his brother, because they work really well together. That brother is the next killer to rear his ugly head, and his name is Fear.

Think of Doubt as a fire and Fear as the match which starts it. Fear is the instigator, and what I've found is that his weapon of choice isn't material. What he carries is much more dangerous than a gun or a knife. He carries lies. I once heard a pastor describe fear as an acronym. False Evidence Appearing Real.

When I was 8, I loved going to the public pool with my sisters. Because of my heart condition, swimming was off the list, but I still liked to go to lay out in the sun, eat candy, and wade in the shallow end of the pool. They had a high dive, and I loved watching the big kids jump off and do their silly tricks. I imagined what it might feel like flying through the air like that. They made it look so easy. One Saturday afternoon, my sisters were preoccupied, and my curiosity got the best of me.

The stairs to the top of the high dive were incredibly narrow, and kids pushed and clamored to make their way to the top. Once I was in the middle of that ladder, I started to think better of myself. Fear was behind me on the ladder, jabbing his elbow into my back. I was scared, but I kept moving up. Once I finally made it to the top, the diving board might as well have been a high wire. That's how steady my lanky legs were on it. I'm sure I looked ridiculous with both arms out balancing myself while I shimmied my feet forward until I reached the edge. *Oo oo wait.* It was a lot higher up than I thought. I could hear all the kids yelling at me to go. I was terrified. Shaking and utterly terrified.

Caroline Klug

I tried to turn around and go back down, but the stairs were too narrow, and the kids were impatient. I shuffled back out there and looked over the edge.

I am going to die.

The truth is, I wasn't going to die, but I *thought* I was, so that tainted my whole experience. I'll sum this story up by saying it ended with a lot of screaming, flailing arms, and a red belly. Oh, and a lifeguard who would have much rather kept talking to the cute boy who was flirting with her than rescuing a drowning 8-year-old. I guess this could be one for the humility books as well.

To this day, I'm afraid of heights. Maybe not so much the height, as the falling from it part. All it takes is one fall to condition you for a lifetime of fear; it's a stronghold that's difficult to break. The more you entertain it, the worse it gets. Sometimes, the only answer is to push past it. This isn't easy, because Fear is scary looking... unlike our next killer, whose appearance is very deceiving.

If I had to equate this one to something living, it would be the Slow Loris. No, I'm not talking about someone's grandma. I'm talking about a small critter that weighs less than two pounds, and looks like it belongs on the cover of a children's book. In reality, this Ewok look-alike can secrete a venom powerful enough to kill you. Welcome to the next up in the list of most wanted: Fantasy.

Creating an alternate reality can be very dangerous. Look at the dangers of role-playing among kids. Their fantasies can become reality in their mind, until they reach the point of delusions. The same goes for us. Our delusions open us up to opportunities until they become fully grown sin.

Tell Them

I'm going to get to the heart of it. Are you daydreaming about someone who isn't your spouse? Are you playing out alternate realities in your head thinking there's no harm because you're not actually *doing* anything? Lies. All lies. Straight from the pit. Every thought you entertain is a real, live manifestation of your heart. You are dangerously perverting something God intended for good.

> "As it is written: 'I have made you a father of many nations.' He is our father in the sight of God, in whom he believed – the God who gives life to the dead and calls into being things that were not." Romans 4:17

God has the power to bring about things that don't already exist – things we may view as impossible. In this passage, Abraham is believing in something God promised him, even though he doesn't have any logical reason to believe it can happen. When you live in your fantasies, you are treating something that doesn't exist as though it does. You're allowing real feelings to be generated from unreal experiences. The only thing you're doing, besides living a lie in your head, is making yourself more vulnerable and susceptible to opportunities the devil will place in front of you in response to those daydreams. You are not only stacking the wood for Satan, but you're pouring some gasoline on it as well. He's just waiting patiently for enough wood and gas before he lights it up. And make no mistake – Satan will wait until you are standing over the top of it.

Fantasy should probably get its own chapter, really. It's a real problem, and one of those insidious ones that creep up on you over time and strangle the life out of you. I should know. It was one of my primary attackers. Mental fantasies played a significant role in my poor decision making. What I first saw as a harmless means to escape to something more fulfilling, *just for fun*, was a slow fade to death. I played scenarios out in my mind, and the acceptance of those scenarios made me dangerously open to the real thing. When opportunity made itself known, I was already halfway there, mentally. It was an easy jump to go the rest of the way.

I have a vivid imagination, and I've learned to use my powers for good. I've learned to indulge in fantasies that please God. I take a lesson from Abraham and I dream about the things He's placed in my heart. I marvel at the ways they could come to pass, though I'm careful not to box God into my ideas. I often like to play a game where I think about all the ways God could bring something to pass. Then, I smile as I assume it will be *none* of those ways, and will be something I had never considered. That's just how He rolls. I have come to *love* how He can surprise me.

I don't struggle with sexual thoughts about other people anymore. That might sound like I'm just saying what I'm supposed to say, but I really don't. I'm sure it helps that I'm married to a gorgeous muscle monster, as I like to call him, who does a great job of loving me. But if you are struggling in this area, I have a suggestion for you. Try using your powers for good and turn your husband into the main character of your fantasies. This does a couple of things. First, it shifts your thoughts away from what is unhealthy and onto what is yours. Second, because those fantasies can be powerful, they have the ability to help you reconnect with intimate feelings and desires for your husband.

Even though he doesn't need any help, I still find myself indulging in thoughts of Jim now and then. It's really, really fun to fanaticize about your husband, because you get all of the gratification and none of the guilt. And it certainly makes me shoot for an earlier bedtime. *Eh-hem.* With all that said, please be wise and take what I'm saying in the spirit I'm saying it in. We can take the most well-intended thoughts and let them get marred by impurities and things that are not pleasing to God. So use the common sense the good Lord gave you, and keep your thoughts inside the God-honoring guardrails.

Let's move on to the scar-face of serial killers. The one you can see coming from a mile away, whose face makes you cringe.

> "Do not judge, or you too will be judged. For in the same way you judge others, you will be judged, and with the measure you use, it will be measured to you." Matthew 7:1-2

This scar face is Judgement. We read the story of an adulteress brought to Jesus in the temple courts (John 8:1-11). The law dictated the woman be stoned, and the Scribes and Pharisees tried to trap Jesus in this. Jesus' response was to ask the person with no sin to throw the first stone at her. If you notice, He never asked for those who had never committed adultery to throw the first stone. He simply said those who had never sinned. God doesn't differentiate between our sins, so we shouldn't either. We shouldn't look at someone and think we are any better or holier just because the wrongs we've committed might be less concerning in society's eyes. Like we talked about in Chapter 1, we are called to love, and leave the judgement seat to God (James 4:12).

Caroline Klug

If you are in the business of comparing mud, just remember – Jesus tells us having an adulterous thought is the same as doing it (Matthew 5:27-28). I sure hope that isn't the same with murder. (Just kidding.)

Let's wrap this up by introducing our final killer in the lineup. This one comes in a pair. They are the Bonnie and Clyde of Satan's front line. They pack a lot of heat, and go by the names of Desensitization and Compromise. Desensitization is the small and pretty one. She walks with a limp, which makes her seem less intimidating, and you think you can handle her. Little by little, she lures you away from safety, until you find yourself standing out in the open. That's when she turns, gives Clyde a nod, and he pulls out his sawed-off Winchester 10-gauge lever-action shotgun and takes aim at you. Compromise is a killing machine, and He doesn't care who he hurts. After all, he's just having fun, and trying to impress his girlfriend.

I can't say enough about the role Compromise played in taking me from joy to destruction. I walked you through some of the compromises I made during the affair, and I hope you can see the train wreck left by my own acceptance of what Desensitization was whispering in my ear. Compromise starts in your mind and squeezes your soul. The more you compromise, the more you justify, and the more *areas* of your life you make compromises in. It's a fast-spreading weed, and if left unmanaged, will strangle the life out of the living things it grows around, namely you.

These are just a handful of the notorious faces which make up Satan's army. There are many more, and they are all hard at work. By the time I got through my decade of disaster, I had eluded most of them. However, some of these serial killers were still stalking me. Let's see which ones.

Chapter 14

$10,000

$10,000. That's what I spent getting a tummy tuck. If I were a betting woman, I'd wager at least a few of you – probably *most* of you – had at least one judgmental thought about why I had that done. I get it. Five years ago, I probably would have thought something like that sounded completely shallow and stuffed full of self-esteem issues. Not to mention the fact that, in my mind, the only women who had things like that done were characters in shows that started with "The Real Housewives of..."

I'd like to tell you what led me to this decision, and why I will never again judge another woman (or man) for having cosmetic surgery. This is also going to be one of those chapters where I talk out of two sides of my face, because there are some things I do regret.

For those who have had the privilege of having a baby, you are well acquainted with what is commonly referred to as a "baby pouch." This is all the skin and scar tissue that's left sagging on your lower abdomen after you've given birth. You know, that time when the skin around your belly spent nine months stretching like Elastigirl on *The Incredibles*?

Caroline Klug

Have you ever taken a damp shirt out of the washer, stretched it out a little, and then let it dry? It never quite goes back to the shape it was when you bought it. Now, the right side of the hem is sagging more than the left, and one section right in the middle suddenly has this strange bulge in it like it dried with your fist in it. *How did that even happen?*

And whose bright idea was it to call it a baby pouch? First of all, it's not a pouch. I couldn't carry anything around in it. If I could, I might have reconsidered removing it for the benefit of functionality, but it was about as useful as the egg separator I finally donated to Goodwill. Second, even if someone did think it was a pouch, it certainly wasn't a *baby* pouch. Kyra wasn't in my skin and tissue. She was in my uterus, which seemed to find its way back to normal size once the pregnancy circus was over. *Why couldn't you, Integumentary System?*

Many women are fortunate not to experience this, but to those of us not so fortunate, it can be a source of both embarrassment and discomfort. It's like waking up one day and finding rickety wooden scaffolding protruding from the side of your house that you neither authorized nor expected. Oh, and it has become a permanent fixture against your smooth vinyl siding. *Uh uh. Nope. Can I get a receipt for that?*

But you know what? After I got through digesting the initial change to my body, I had made peace with it because I chose to look at it as a reminder of the beautiful daughter I had. I still didn't like how I felt in dress pants, but I learned to deal with it and accept it as the new normal.

Unfortunately, my baby pouch was at the center of the target of that verbally abusive man from the prior chapters. There was one horrible night when he was, unbeknown to me, high on whatever pain killer he took and couldn't perform sexually. As was his way, he immediately began to berate me and tell me why it was my fault, because I couldn't do it for him. He must have been especially angry that night, because he did something I have only told one person about, until now. With both hands, he grabbed the saggy part of the skin on my belly, and for the next thirty seconds, or what felt like thirty minutes in my mind, while he was still gripping and shaking it, he told me how utterly disgusting that saggy skin was to him, and how utterly disgusting *I* was to him. He let it go and stormed out of the bedroom.

Embarrassment doesn't even begin to cover what I felt. Neither does mortified. Looking back on that moment, I honestly don't even know where to start when dissecting the complicated web of emotional lines, all sticking to each other and making an even bigger mess as you try to pull it apart. I didn't know about the drugs at the time, so I thought he was telling the truth. Even if his truth was distorted, it was still real in his mind that I was disgusting. That my body was disgusting. I didn't know how to even process that. If something like that happened today, I'd probably punch him in the face and break his nose so he could have something really disgusting to look at. But back then, I didn't have it in me. I didn't have the courage to stand up for myself. Instead, I just cried and felt ugly. I didn't know how to make it better. I couldn't change how I looked.

Or could I?

This is a tough bone for me to exhume, but I can't help anyone else who might be struggling if I'm not real about struggling with it myself. Remember how I said insecurity can cause reckless thinking, which in turn can cause reckless behavior? Well, reckless behavior is exactly what happened in response to this. I became obsessed with trying to lose weight quickly. I figured if I tried hard enough – shocked my body significantly enough – that maybe I *could* make this go away, and then I wouldn't be disgusting anymore.

That's when it started. When I started making myself throw up after each meal. It felt horrible and I hated doing it, but I thought it was the only quick answer. For the better part of several months, I would throw up one or two of my meals every day. Every. Single. Day. That is significant trauma to your body with devastating long-term effects.

Dehydration, fatigue, heartburn, inflamed esophagus, menstruation issues, sore throat, food aversion, abnormalities in taste, and heart failure. Yes, heart failure, said the girl with a history of heart defects. Those are just *some* of the physical side effects. Now let's look at mental and emotional side effects. Anxiety, depression, low self-esteem, guilt, and mood swings. Do any one of those sound helpful to what I was already feeling? That's like burying a person in rocks and then dumping wet cement over the top of it all.

I lost weight, all right. Everywhere but where I wanted to lose it most. I looked sick, but I had hoped being skinnier everywhere else would compensate for my belly.

Of course it didn't, because that wasn't the problem. It was never the problem. The real problem was always how I felt about myself.

I'm going to be very honest with you. Just now, I stopped writing and I cried. I cried for this girl I used to be, who was hurting so badly she didn't know of another way to gain acceptance other than hurting herself even more. I cried as my heart hurt for so many other people out there who are living this nightmare right now. It's not just the nightmare of what they are doing to their bodies. It's the nightmare of *why* they are doing it. They see so little value in themselves, they justify their behavior as the only way to be what they think someone else needs them to be. The end that justifies the means. But to *what* end?

Sweet One, if you are struggling with this very real problem called bulimia, I pray you will get real with yourself. What end game are you trying to justify? Feeling attractive to someone who refuses to treat you with the love and respect you deserve? There is no benefit worth the sacrifice of your self-worth.

You will only find confidence in who Christ made you to be. Take it from someone who's tried – there is nothing on the face of this earth that will fill the black hole of a void that was only meant to be filled by God. No earthly thing or person can fill what was designed to be filled supernaturally.

I stopped making myself throw up when that relationship ended, and when God really got a hold of me and told me I needed to make a choice. I promised Him in that moment I would never again make myself throw up food. I'm happy to say I've kept that promise, but I've carried the shame of my actions around with me for way too long. So there it is. I lay it humbly at your feet and hope you can take my words to heart and allow them to change you in the ways I didn't used to have to courage to allow.

For a long time, I accepted my body as it was. I had made a lot of progress in my spiritual walk, and that translated to a healthy dose of Christ-centered self-esteem. Although I was feeling good about myself, I started thinking about things I could change for the better for myself. Not for someone else, but for *me*. I had made peace with my body, but I desired to feel better in my clothing. I was in my late thirties when I first started thinking about the option of getting an abdominoplasty. It was an elective cosmetic surgery, so nothing was covered under insurance. As a single mom, it was a big decision, to spend that kind of money on something that was technically unnecessary. Thankfully, God had blessed me with a good job that allowed me to own a house and build my savings. Regardless of that, I still stewed about it for some time. When it comes to big purchases, I tend to overthink, and then think some more.

One of the hesitations swirling around in my mind was if I had done the work. Had I done everything I could physically to lean and tone my body, to see how much of it could go away on its own? Now, I well recalled how little that changed when I struggled with bulimia, but I couldn't help but wonder if anything would change if I did things the right way. The *healthy* way. I made a decision that I was going to diligently pursue good health and fitness, and re-evaluate my desire for surgery once I got to the point where I knew any additional work would reap no additional benefits.

The year I turned 40 was that point. I had been working hard, and was in the best shape of my life. I was running half-marathons and strength training several times per week. I looked good and I felt great. But I still had to work my attire choices around my scaffolding. I started doing the research and overthinking it some more. Do you notice, I didn't say *praying* some more?

It was toward the end of that same summer when I met Jim. I'll be saving that story for a later chapter, so I'll fast forward through all the love and butterflies to when we had a serious conversation about this. The seriousness was more in the form of me coming to him and telling him what I was thinking about doing. We were not married at the time, or even engaged yet, and although this decision was ultimately mine, I wanted to know what he thought.

Although we had not been together long, Jesus had already given me a glimpse into his amazing heart, and I knew how this conversation was going to go but, in the spirit of transparency, I think a huge subconsciously nervous part of me wanted to know if he'd jump on the train. Would he *encourage* me to have the surgery because I'd look better? And no, that would definitely *not* be what I wanted to hear.

Emotional issues you haven't fully dealt with have a tendency to follow you around like a wart. If you don't take the proper steps to remove it completely, it will just keep coming back. I had that discussion with the intent of unification, but I know I was also addressing an old fear.

My fear was pushed aside, as that conversation went exactly how I expected it to. He listened as I told him what I was thinking and explained the reasons I was thinking about it. He asked a few questions. Then, in no uncertain terms, made it very clear to me that this was not anything I should be doing for him. If it was, it was completely unnecessary. He thought I was beautiful, and loved me just the way I was.

Within another few months, I decided it was something I wanted to do for myself, so I went through the steps and set the appointments. I was at my pre-op appointment, listening as one of the surgical nurses walked me through the procedure so I knew what to expect. She made it sound easy breezy, and I was ready to do this.

I've had a lot of surgeries in my life. Heart surgery, foot surgery, my appendix removed, an ovary removed, and of course, my C-Section when I had Kyra. From a physical recovery standpoint, nothing, and I mean nothing, was worse than this tummy tuck. I would gladly go through the recovery of a foot surgery again, over that cluster.

If you get squeamish with regard to medical procedures, you might just want to squint your eyes a bit and skim quickly through the next page or so. I'm going to get graphic about the procedure and recovery because, for starters, I wish someone else would have with me. But also, because it plays into a part of the deeper message I want to share.

I'm not educated enough on the matter to tell you what's typical, but I can tell you my experience included two major things. The first was the actual tummy tuck, where the surgeon removes excess skin and fat from your abdomen. This involved making a twelve-inch incision (I measured it) horizontally across the entire width of my lower abdomen. So, ladies, if you think you'll walk away from this procedure with your vinyl siding looking unscathed, think again. The scar is so long, it looks more like a freak shark accident where doctors were miraculously able to stitch my lower half back into place. Once the incision is made, excess fat is removed, and the skin on both sides of the incision is pulled taut together, so the surgeon knows how much to remove.

Side note. I had my appendix removed the summer before I started college. I had a small scar from one of the incisions they made and, when I was pregnant with Kyra and my belly expanded, that scar stretched into a really cool replica of the one Harry Potter has on his forehead. Except I had it first. *Neener neener, Harry.* It was my lightning bolt, and it was awesome. The morning of my surgery, when I was standing naked while the doctor drew all over me with his surgical marker (not at all awkward), I showed him that scar on my stomach and asked him to try to avoid removing it, if at all possible. I really wanted to keep it because it reminded me of all the positive reasons for my body changing.

Back to the freak show. Because there was so much excess skin above the incision that needed to get pulled down, I lost my belly button.

Yeah, I know. I had the same reaction. Go ahead and take a minute for yourself.

Good thing he's done a lot of these, because he made me a brand spanking new one. New isn't always better. Sometimes new is just, well, different. Okay, it wasn't just different, it was a little weird. It mostly looks like a belly button, but it doesn't *feel* the same. The edges of normal, God-given belly buttons are stretchy and pliable feeling. The edges of my artificially constructed knock-off belly button are rigid and not at all stretchy, which makes washing in there more tedious. Add the fact that the nerves in that part of my stomach never came back, which means there's no feeling, and I have to be especially careful not to pull too hard, lest I rip it.

Before he closed the incision, he did the second procedure. After a woman carries a baby, often the abdominal muscles in her stomach will pull apart a bit. This is generally not a big deal, but it makes it a lot more difficult to ever attain six pack status, if you're going for that kind of thing. When he initially asked me if I wanted him to stitch them tighter together, I really should have taken a play out of the "supermodel Christie Brinkley has bangs and layers" playbook and said no thank you. But the thought of having a six pack when I had never before achieved such a profound accomplishment, sounded too impressive to pass up.

Yeah, man, do it up.

With my permission, he pulled those muscles back in tight to center and sewed them together. He then closed the incision. Yes, you feel this after. A lot.

I wish I could say that was it. Oh, sweet mercy, how I wish that was the end. This next part is the part that still makes me shudder. When you do this procedure, there's apparently a lot of fluid that collects in your abdominal region. To allow for proper drainage and healing, plastic tubes about two or three centimeters wide are inserted into both groins. These tubes float inside your abdomen to collect the fluids. Fluids move out of your body through the tubes, down into small plastic bottles attached to the opposite ends of each tube. These need to be emptied out one or two times per day.

Are you drawing this picture in your mind with me? My entire mid-section felt like someone poured gasoline on it, lit it on fire, put it out with a chainsaw, then poured some salt on it for good measure. As if that were not bad enough, I have physical tubes jutting out from both of my groins collecting fluid that looked like the off-yellow color of my brother's socks in grade school. And these tubes had to stay in for *weeks*. I wouldn't wish that surgery on my worst enemy.

Why am I telling you all of this? Because trying to get through transformation can be excruciating. And if you force it, it will be way more painful than it needs to be. There are several reasons I don't regret going through with it. I did this for me, and I *do* feel a lot better about how my pants and swimsuits fit on me. Right or wrong, it has helped to boost my confidence. For that reason, you won't find me judging people anymore, knowing every person has a story, and I can't know what's right for them.

But there is something I do regret. I don't believe I was completely healed from some of my past trauma when I made the decision to do this. A part of me looked at this procedure as the final step of that healing, which was to remove it out of view. I don't think that was the healthy way to go about it. Simply removing something out of view feels more like a shortcut through the critical work. I wish I would have been able to make the decision to have that done without an ounce of it being about what anyone else thought of it, or uncomfortable feelings about what anyone in my past thought about it. The only person that mattered was Jim, and he had already told me it wasn't even a blip on his radar.

There is one more thing I regret. I wish I had not ignored one of the obvious red flags of being ready to move forward with this. Secrecy. I was afraid for even the people closest to me to know I had this done. I was afraid of being judged, and a part of me was just plain ol' embarrassed to admit I even had it. Whenever we do anything in the dark, that should be an obvious indicator that we're headed the wrong way, or it's simply not the right timing. Allowing God to bring healing in His way and in His timing is always the better method. If you can find peace there first, then all the power to you to have that butt lift.

Note to self: just because the doctor stitches your abs back together, doesn't mean you'll wake up with a six pack. You *still* have to do the work.

Caroline Klug

Chapter 15
Who Told You That?

We just spent some time talking about why I chose to have a tummy tuck. Most of it was for myself, but some of it was to stop the voices from my past, still squatting illegally in my head. I tried to have surgically removed what I really needed God to emotionally remove. This brings us to a very important question.

Whose voice are you listening to?

Most people are at least familiar with the story of Adam and Eve in the Garden of Eden (Genesis 3). Adam and Eve were God's first created human beings, and they had it made. As if it wasn't cool enough that they got to actually walk around *with* God, they had this beautiful garden surrounding them, filled with everything their hearts could need or desire, including the beauty of each other. They wanted for nothing. Or so they thought.

There are a lot of bad things that happen in the world, but I think most of us, especially those of us in America, can say we have it pretty good. One of Satan's go-to tricks is to manipulate us into thinking we need *more*. He uses Comparison to whisper lies that what we have isn't enough, even when what we have is, by all the world's standard, excess. That's exactly what he did to Adam and Eve in that garden. God gave them free use of everything except for the fruit off *one* tree. Adam and Eve didn't seem to mind this before Satan entered the picture, so we have to assume they were fine with it. However, Satan appears and starts whispering all the reasons they *should* want it, including telling them if they eat it, they will be able to know the difference between good and evil, like God (Genesis 3:5). By nature of his words, he's getting Adam and Eve to compare themselves to God, and get them to want what He has. And look carefully at his crafty words. What he says isn't necessarily a lie, for eating that fruit did open their eyes. However, he twisted what God said, and made them believe they would be gaining power rather than death.

That's how Satan works.

Adam and Eve bought into the lies of Satan and ate the fruit. Once they did, it says their eyes were opened, they realized they were naked, and they used fig leaves to cover their private parts. Okay, first, I'd like to know if Satan was also responsible for identifying which parts were *private*. If so, couldn't he at least have done us a solid by telling them the hair on their heads was a private part? Covering that up could have saved me a lot of hassle in middle school, and a lot of time as an adult. Or what about feet? Feet are not beautiful. They need help. Especially guy feet.

Guys, it is *not* sexy when you let your toenails grow past the tip of your toe. Nor is it acceptable to say this is by design so you can play the guitar with your feet like Jimi Hendrix.

Tell Them

Back to the idiots who ate the fruit. *My dearest ancestors, did you not realize how great you had it? Did you not think about the ramifications of being doomed to a lifetime of having to decide what to wear every day? Of course you didn't.* The fruit was probably shiny and looked delicious. Satan is smart and patient. He probably approached them right before dinner. When desire meets opportunity, we can get stupid. We think with the wrong parts of our body and make decisions too quickly. And sometimes that wrong part isn't always a naughty part. Sometimes it's our stomach. When desire is thrown into the mixing bowl, we ought to spend a few more minutes thinking things through.

The Bible tells us Eve was the first to be convinced the forbidden fruit would be good for her, so she took some and ate it. Then, she handed it over to her husband to eat.

Hold up.

When we don't think things through, we can be ignorant to the consequences of our actions. And when we're ignorant, we usually drag other people along for the ride. Nobody likes to go to a party alone, especially when our inner voice is trying to justify it. And seeing someone else do what we're doing might make it okay. Our actions are not just about us. They are about every person we influence and drag down with us. We have to recognize we can use our powers of influence for good or evil.

All of this aside, there's a very interesting sentence in this story that's easily overlooked, but packed full of meaning.

> "Then the man and his wife heard the sound of the Lord God as He was walking in the garden in the

> cool of the day, and they hid from the Lord God among the trees of the garden. But the Lord God called to the man, 'Where are you?' He answered, 'I heard You in the garden, and I was afraid because I was naked; so I hid.' And He said, 'Who told you that you were naked? Have you eaten from the tree that I commanded you not to eat from?'" Genesis 3:8-11

There are actually *two* really interesting questions in here, but we'll start with the first. God asked them who told them they were naked. Make no mistake. God is not asking because He doesn't know. He's asking because He wants *them* to say it out loud. He wants them to acknowledge the source of their knowledge did not come from Him, but from the enemy. When I look back at the lies behind so many of the horrible decisions I made, I probably could have titled this book, Who Told You That? It took me way too long to mature enough to ask myself that question. Now I'm going to ask you.

That lie you're believing about yourself, your life, or your future... who told you that?

When processing information, we must always consider the source. Remember all those scars on my face after being mauled by the German shepherd? They faded a bit by the time I got into high school, but I still had one that was very visible, which was long and extended upwards from the top right side of my lip.

I was very insecure about it as a teenager. One day, a boy I had a crush on made fun of it, and I went home crying, feeling completely devastated and ugly. My dad asked me

Tell Them

why I was crying and I told him. Even though the dog was well trained, I can only imagine my dad felt responsible. Right or wrong, as a parent, I would. I share this, because, after I came home that day feeling broken, I'm certain it's the reason he offered to take me to a cosmetic surgeon to see about getting it removed. This would be an elective procedure, and not at all in their budget.

What's interesting to me is the notion that my dad already gave me a beautiful gift with regard to those scars. His prayers. Remember that renowned plastic surgeon who happened to be in the right place at the right time when I came into the Emergency Room? If I were a gambling woman, I would bet that gift was in response to the prayers God knew Dad would offer up as they rushed me to the hospital. As a parent, I'm sure his first prayer was for my life, but I bet the second would be for God to minimize the visual damage so I wouldn't hurt emotionally from what he surely thought was his mistake. God answered both that day. Although I did have some visible scars, the damage could have been so much worse, had a less experienced doctor been sewing me back together.

We actually went back to that same plastic surgeon for a consultation, and he explained how he would cut out the scar and re-stitch it so it wasn't nearly as visible. Once I got home, I can still vividly remember sitting on my bed and feeling an immense sense of comfort. I don't think I realized it was God speaking to me at the time, but after that moment, I went to my dad and said,

"Dad, I really appreciate you being willing to do this for me, but this scar is a part of who I am and a part of my story. And if some boy thinks it makes me ugly, then that boy isn't the right boy for me." I can't explain how such mature words came out of me, outside of God healing that wounded part of my heart. Today, I don't even see that scar anymore, and if I do happen to notice it, I have zero hurt associated with it. To me, it's as distinctive as my green eyes. It's just part of what makes up my face.

Who told me the scar on my face made me ugly? Some boy who would probably never realize the impact of his words until he was a father. Which he is today. (I know this because Mark Zuckerberg tells us everything.) The point is, the source of that information wasn't a credible witness to the truth of who I was. And that source certainly didn't have all the facts, because he clearly didn't take what was on the *inside* of me into consideration. Was I going to base my self-worth on what a 16-year-old boy said, or what God said?

Lies and injustice come in a lot of different shapes and sizes. As I write, I'm sitting in a Starbucks and listening to a very old song that reminds me of someone. This person has a lot to her personality that I'm not sure she always sees. She's very funny and talented, but she's also really smart. Always has been. But somewhere along the lines, someone told her she wasn't. Someone who was hurting, hurt her, and her self-worth has paid the price ever since. That hits my justice button hard, because I see a person who can do whatever she puts her mind to. She is quickly wounded by other people's words, even if they're joking, and I think it's because she's never fully healed from the old cassette tapes that played over and over in her mind when she was younger – the lies someone else made her believe about herself. She had been the unfortunate recipient of some of those crap sandwiches life serves now and then, and I'm sure the taste of them are still in her mouth. I pray all the time that God will help her consider the source, and allow her to see herself as He does.

How do you see yourself? If any of those views are unhealthy, who are the 16-year-old boys in your life who are feeding you that bad information? You need to find them, throat punch them, and leave them sitting on their keesters. Okay, maybe don't throat punch them. Especially if they're 16 and you're over 18. That would be really bad, and you'd probably need a lawyer. Maybe just give them a good talking-to instead.

In all seriousness, it's critically important we know the source of our identity. For years, I looked for mine in all the wrong places. I stood on a street corner with a sign that said, "Will perform for validation." I compromised my beliefs and morals because I thought it was the only way to feel valued. Satan manipulated me into fearing it was the only way to obtain acceptance. I was so busy *doing*, I didn't stop long enough to pray and understand what my Father had already made clear to me through His Word. He wants to make it clear to you, too:

> "For You created my inmost being; You knit me together in my mother's womb. I praise You because I am fearfully and wonderfully made; Your works are wonderful, I know that full well. My frame was not hidden from You when I was made in the secret place, when I was woven together in the depths of the earth. Your eyes saw my unformed body; all the days ordained for me were written in Your book before one of them came to be." Psalm 139:13-16

Caroline Klug

Chosen One, you were no accident. You were carefully planned, tenderly created, and generously loved. God didn't put you on this earth to perform for your love like an animal in the Barnum and Bailey Circus. He put you here to love Him and *be* loved by Him. No strings attached. Life does give us a few rings of fire now and then, but rest assured your Father loves you the same on either side of that ring.

It took me a *long* time to stop trying to overcome feelings of rejection by compromising myself for the perceived reward of love and acceptance. It was a mirage that left me thirstier than before I started my trek.

> "Jesus answered, 'Everyone who drinks this water will be thirsty again, but whoever drinks the water I give them will never thirst. Indeed, the water I give them will become in them a spring of water welling up to eternal life.'" John 4:13

Jesus is referring to salvation in this Scripture, but there is so much more. His love, for starters. What I thought I had to work for, God wanted to give me for free. I only needed to accept the love of my Father, which was there for me. The. Whole. Time. He was standing at the well just waiting for me to ask Him for the only drink which could truly satisfy my cravings – Him. Once I fully understood and accepted that, my heart and life underwent the kind of transformation no earthly surgeon would ever be capable of.

My reliance on job performance and status had been growing, but so was my faith in God, and that presented me with a *new* conflict. A *good* conflict. God didn't want my identity being rooted in anything but Him, and for good reason. As my faith and knowledge of His Word grew, so did my self-confidence. I started seeing and believing what *God* said about me, rather than what any of those people who hurt me said. That changed my behavior, because it changed *me* as a person, from the heart-side out, as I like to say.

When your identity and value are rooted in Christ, it changes how you see yourself, and how you see others. It gives you a right perspective. God is a heart God. He cares more about what happens *in* you than what happens *to* you. And once we get centered on Him, He has a funny way of giving us the desires of our hearts. That is, taking His desires and planting them deep within our own hearts, so we are perfectly and beautifully aligned (Psalm 37:4).

There's a saying that says something about finding love when you least expect it. I didn't find the right love until I went through that heart and life transformation, and took the focus off myself and put it on God. Prior to that, I was looking for it like my dog looks for scraps when I'm cooking. *Pip, stop licking the floor. You're embarrassing yourself.* It wasn't until I was content that the magic really happened. I was ready. I was *finally* ready.

Caroline Klug

Chapter 16

The Years the Locusts Ate

When I finally came to grips with writing this book, my focus shifted to Jim. Because of the invasive amount of personal information I would be sharing, I knew aligning on this would be important. We are partners in everything, and this was no exception. I wanted to know how he felt about it. Would he be embarrassed by some of the things I'd be sharing about my past? Would he worry about how it might reflect on him? Would he willingly handle the questions he might get from friends and outsiders alike? So, we talked. I explained what the book was and the kinds of things that would be in it. I told him I promised God nothing would be out of scope, and asked him how he'd feel about that. With zero hesitation he said,

"You do whatever God's telling you to do. I'm fine."

I thanked him for understanding, to which he replied with something that made us both giggle. *He is the king of levity.* I knew that's how he would respond, but hearing it still made me fall just a little more in love with him, if that's even possible. Welcome to a very tender part of my love story. One that never fails to bring me to tears.

> "'Even now,' declares the Lord, 'return to Me with all your heart, with fasting and weeping and mourning.' Rend your heart and not your garments. Return to the Lord your God, for He is gracious and compassionate, slow to anger and abounding in love, and He relents from sending calamity." Joel 2:12-13

When I got on my knees after that last affair and begged God to help me get out of it, like a lost and scared child aching for the love of her Father's arms, I laid it all bare before Him. My sin. My failures. My pain. My shame. I lay wounded, sobbing, and unable to move. As you know, He honored that visceral cry of my heart. Jesus crawled into the pit with me, picked me up, and carried me out. He brought me back to the other ninety-nine.

Lean in a little, because what I'm about to say is vital to my love story. It's vital to you understanding *your* love story and it's critical to understanding why God is what the Bible says He is... love.

God didn't just help me out of my pit and forgive me. He didn't just welcome me back into His flock. He went about a million steps further and gave me above and beyond anything my sinful self could ever dream to deserve. After everything I had done. It was like taking the Toyota out for a joy ride and crashing it, and He turns around and gives me a Ferrari.

> "I will repay you for the years the locusts have eaten – the great locust and the young locust, the other locusts and the locust swarm – My great army that I sent among you." Joel 2:25

Tell Them

In order to explain this verse about the locusts, I'd like to introduce to you to a dog Jim and I recently adopted from a rescue, whom I mentioned in the last chapter. Her name is Pip, and she's a 10-year-old Chiweenie. That's part Chihuahua and part Dachshund (aka, wiener dog). Jim won't let me call her a Chiweenie in public. He prefers to tell people she's a baby Chupacabra. A mythical, blood sucking, dog-like beast. All twelve pounds of her. *It's better for his manhood.*

Prior to coming to us, Pip spent her days locked in a travel carrier; one so small she couldn't fully stand up. She sat in her carrier and watched as two other large dogs got run of the house and yard. This went on not for days, but for years. She must not have been let out to pee much, because this girl has a bladder of steel. I guess that's a sad fringe benefit. For years that poor little dog was confined to a prison while she watched other dogs do what she wished she could do. Pip is one of the most loving little dogs I have ever met. She adores human contact and loves her humans unconditionally. She's extremely calm, tolerant, and obedient. I look at her some days and wonder how in the world anyone could want to stuff her away somewhere.

Jim and I are big water people. We live on the river and often take our boat down to the City Deck in downtown Green Bay. We also have a sailboat in Door County that we spend almost every weekend on in the summer. This was an important factor in deciding whether or not to adopt Pip. We wanted to make sure she was comfortable within our lifestyle. The first night we fostered her, we walked her out onto the docks, put her into the river boat, and went for a little ride. It was the first time I saw her light up and come into herself. She looked like the queen of that boat! She loved it. *Checkmark.* Then we brought her to the sailboat for the weekend. That dog is seaworthy! She loved that too. *Checkmark.* We were elated, and went through with the adoption the day we got back from the sailboat.

Now, Pip has a fabulous life. When she's not lying next to me while I write, she's sitting out on the deck looking out over the river and bossing all the river critters. She gets ample love and affection and, something that tenders my heart, a whole lot of fresh air. Whenever Pip is in her happy place, she grins. Yes, she grins. It's a wide mouth smile with her eyes half shut, and it just screams, "I love my life." And who wouldn't, when every day starts with a belly rub? This started sometime within the first couple of weeks of having her. Every morning when we get out of bed, Pip is so excited, and wags her tail with such force, her whole back end swings from side to side, causing her to walk sideways. Then she throws herself dramatically down and rolls onto her back so we can rub her belly. And if we stop too soon, she makes a grunting sound, nudges our hand with her nose, and rolls onto her back again, waiting for more love.

Pip had a rough start in life, and her being in our home is an opportunity for her last years to be better than the sum of her first ten. And that's exactly how I feel about what God did for me. I hope I can do this next part justice, because it's important.

Hurting One, even if you feel like your choices or circumstances have robbed you of years or even decades, God, in all His infinite power, can make the time in front of you so full of blessings that it outweighs the years you felt were lost. The years *you* were lost. There will be so much joy, it will feel as though that time was returned to you. You see, we might not have receipts for all those bad things we want to return, but God does. He's been holding onto them the entire time, waiting to exchange any and every bad thing for what is good and pure and merciful and loving.

In Pip's case, she didn't do anything to deserve those hard-life knocks. I've had a few of those undeserved knocks too, but I did a lot of knocking myself, and I'm here to tell you firsthand that God's mercy runs deeper than any ocean and higher than any star in His universe. Don't ever think your past will limit your future. The only thing that can limit your future is your own thinking.

After Jesus climbed into that pit with me, everything changed. Most importantly, my heart. The love of God wasn't just something I read about or even *kind of* felt. It was a sea I was free diving in. I saw things I had never seen before. I saw the heart of God, and it was beyond beautiful. I can't help but think about all those years ago when God led me to the doctor who fixed my physical heart. He knew there was so much more work to heal my spiritual heart, and it would take a decade before I was ready for *that* surgery. That doctor may have altered the electrical pathways of my heart, but ten years later, God transformed the very beats of my heart.

Only then, and after a time of healing, was I truly ready to receive the gift I didn't deserve, but would forever be changed by. Little did I know, that gift of mine was on *his* knees, getting the beats of his own heart transformed. It never ceases to amaze me how God fits the cosmic puzzle so perfectly together.

Jim and I met on Match.com. I had created an account after my heart transformation, and made sure my profile would scare anyone who didn't love Jesus. I started going on a few dates, but didn't really connect the way I wanted to. Then this handsome guy swiped right and sent me a message. After messaging back and forth for a week, we met out for a cocktail. Because you should never commit to something as lengthy as dinner when meeting for the first time. You need a faster out just in case the guy who shows up was using a picture of his son instead. *Just sayin'. It happened.* So I walk in and lock eyes with my future husband. I sometimes wonder if heaven was eating popcorn at the time. We went on our first real date a few days later, and that was that. I knew within weeks Jim was the one I had been praying for all those years. But I had a problem. I was afraid.

Here I was, staring my heart's desire in the face, and I was afraid. I was afraid of going all in only for my heart to get eviscerated. Because that's what *everyone* had done to my heart, so why should Jim be any exception?

Satan winced as he saw the partnership forming. He knew what it would mean for him. For his plans. He hit the button and a loud alarm sounded. Fear and Doubt came scrambling into the room and fell to attention in front of him. Satan pointed his finger at me and they scurried toward me with his words on their lips. They whispered those words to me and it made me cry, run into my bathroom, and sit on the closed toilet seat.

He's not the real deal. You just want him to be.

He's going to cheat on you eventually.

He's going to hurt you like everyone else has.

Tell Them

God smiled as He saw the story that was yet to unfold. He invited Love and Discernment into His Throne room, greeting them each with a hug. God pointed His finger at me and they nodded in understanding. The Holy Spirit carried them over and rested them gently on my heart. Fear and Doubt could not withstand them, and they departed. God called Knowledge into His Throne room, and sent him to me with a special message.

Don't be afraid. Jim is the one. Everything is going to be okay.

That whisper – that neon sign – changed everything. The words of Doubt and Fear were quieted and replaced with the assurance of what was to come. That knowledge was another gift I didn't deserve, but graciously accepted. Joy and Happiness were finally at the same table together, and it felt wonderful. *Sorry, Jim, that it happened while I was sitting on the toilet. You can't choose the moment.*

When God is doing something wonderful in your life, don't think Satan won't keep trying to pull you back into old patterns of thinking. You have to be alert and recognize triggers and sensitivities for what they are. Lies. If you can put a name to it, you can evict it. Seek healing and freedom so past baggage doesn't interfere with the gifts in your life.

I had to deal with a lot of old triggers and sensitivities. I let some of that baggage come into my relationship with Jim. I thank God he is the man he is, because he knew it was bullshit. (Sorry, but that seemed to be the best fitting word.) I will never forget the moment Jim took my face in his hands and told me it was okay if I felt afraid, and that I just needed to let him *show* me why I didn't need to be. I prayed for so many years for a *real* man, and I sure do have one now. *Don't I, Buttercup?*

Okay, so I do this thing where I call Jim affectionate little nicknames that make him feel less manly. I never do it when it's just the two of us. Only in public. Where embarrassment can be maximized. In return, he calls me rude things like Thunder Thighs and Walrus Ass. *Close your mouth. He doesn't really mean it.* He only uses phrases which are ridiculously untrue. I don't exactly have much padding back there.

There was this time Jim, Kyra, and I were at Subway getting lunch. He was over by the counter and I had walked over to the drink machines. Jim yells,

"Hey, Thunder Thighs! Can you get me a water?"

The mouths of the nice couple sitting in the booth in between us hung wide open. Had it not been for my genuine laughter, Kyra thought the man might invite Jim out to the parking lot. I still giggle today, wondering if that couple prays for the poor, mistreated young lady they saw in Subway that one day. Mistreated, I am not.

> "Now that you have purified yourselves by obeying the truth so that you have sincere love for each other, love one another deeply, from the heart." 1 Peter 1:22

We both have our moments. No person can ever be perfect. There are times I get mad at Jim, but it lasts for like five minutes. I can sincerely say we love each other deeply. Gratitude is a powerful thing. One of the upsides of marrying when you're older is, the more you go through, the more you recognize a good thing. I know couples who

Tell Them

have gotten divorced over anger resulting from the man leaving dirty dishes out. I don't always love cleaning up after Jim. *He leaves a lot of dishes out.* But how wonderful that I have someone's dishes to pick up.

Jim is a lot of things I prayed for, and just as many things I didn't even know I needed. God is pretty smart. He listens to the desires of our heart, but He is wise enough to mold what He knows is best into the mix. In past relationships, I thought my extroverted personality should be paired with an equally extroverted partner. What a surprise when God sent me an introvert. But how right He was. Jim has a quiet intelligence I recognized right away, because my dad was the same way. Jim never needs to be the center of attention or the smartest person in the room, but when you talk to him, you realize quickly that he's very well rounded and can speak to a lot of different topics. He's comfortable in his own skin and has nothing to prove. When you ask him what he does, he won't tell you he owns an electrical contracting company. He'll tell you he's an electrician. I love that about him. But what I love so, so much is his quick-fire wit. I said before that he's the king of levity. That man can fire off a witty comment faster than I can blink, and he makes me laugh. Every. Single. Day. That too, is a gift. Be with someone who makes you laugh. It is heart healing.

I'm competent in a lot of things, but I'm kind of old fashioned when it comes to husband and wife roles. I'm quite comfortable being the heart of the home, and I always prayed for a manly man. Someone who could take the bull by the horns and just *handle* something. Whether it's a flat tire, a furnace that won't start, or investigating a late-night noise, I wanted a man who was comfortable figuring it out. Jim is that man. I could tell him a herd of buffalo broke through the wall downstairs and I'm pretty sure there's still a few down there, and he'd say,

"Okay, I'll go take care of that."

My point is, God listens. He gives you what He knows is best, but it's never a coincidence that it's wrapped around the desires of your heart which are God honoring. That was especially evident with one, very specific, desire of my heart.

Ten years ago, I sat in a room at my church watching a Bible study video by a popular Christian speaker. She was talking about how her husband would lay hands on her and pray for her before she would go out on stage and speak. I remember wanting that so badly, that my heart broke into a thousand pieces. My mouth was silent as I watched the video, but my heart was screaming. I knew what God had placed in my heart, ministry-wise, and I told Him my heart's desire for a true partner. One who would be all-in with me. One who would pray for me like that. I wanted it, but I couldn't fathom it. Until now.

It was kind of funny, actually. There was one day, early on in dating when I was telling Jim about something I was going through, and he offered to pray for me. Right then and there. He put his arms around me and we prayed. *It was better than sex.* Yes, I just said that. The next day I saw him, and we prayed together again. Then, the third day, we didn't. I wanted to, and I felt like we should, but I was kind of embarrassed to ask. I got in my car and left, bothered the whole time. As soon as I was no longer driving, I got my phone out, and texted him a prayer. From that day forward, there isn't a day that goes by that we don't pray together. Every morning after we get up, we wrap our arms around each other and we pray. For us, for the business, for my books and readers, for the people we love, for the church we go to, for the community groups we are a part of, for everything. And on those rare occasions we are apart, then we pick up the phone early in the morning, and pray together that way.

God heard me that day, sitting in that room at church. And isn't it just like Him to give more than we ask for? So much more.

I know I've made Jim out to be a superhero. *He kind of is to me.* But he has his kryptonite. Most predominantly, poop. Jim has a severe aversion to dog poop. He would like to call it an allergy. Besides the fact that poop is inherently funny, it's one of the reasons I've strung poop jokes throughout the book. Because seeing Jim's left eye twitch is really funny. *Right, Cuddle Bunny? You're welcome. Love you, too. Just watch a sailing video on YouTube. You'll probably be fine.*

In the spirit of confessions, I'll put one out there that might make Jim want to get *on* that sailboat and sail away. We did have sex before marriage. Not one of our finer God-loving decisions. We justified it in our minds because we knew we were getting married.

Compromise alarm.

See how Satan takes something and spins it? Well, I started feeling a *lot* of conviction. I had no fear of telling Jim this, but we were only a few months away from getting married, so part of me thought it might be stupid to say something at this point. But the conviction continued to press itself on my heart. I was going to talk to him when he came over to my house that night.

I kid you not, with what I'm about to say next. When Jim walked in the door that night, he dropped his workout bag to the floor, looked at me kind of dejectedly, and said,

"We can't sleep together anymore until we're married."

After a wide-eyed moment of silence, I slapped my hands on the couch I was sitting on and said, "Oh, thank God!"

Even though it was only a few months, I'm still thankful we were obedient to the conviction. I wish we could have done a better job with discipline in that department, but what have we been saying? You can only move forward.

I bring up this particular story because I want to pull my soap box out of the fire and get back on it for a second. There's an epidemic lie that says, "try it before you buy it." Because sex is so important in a relationship, people believe they should take that car for a spin before buying it, to make sure it's a good fit. If you are praying about your relationship, and the two of you have received God's confirmation that it's the real deal, then why would your trust stop there? If God put the two of you together, and you're prayerfully confident in His blessing, and the experienced sharing of mental, emotional, and spiritual intimacy, then you can be sure He won't forget about sexual intimacy.

Remember how I said praying together was better than sex? Let me tell you, sharing a spiritual intimacy with someone is better than any other intimacy out there. It can bring you closer, faster than all of them combined. I'm convinced that's because there's something supernaturally magical that happens when two hearts meet before God's. Instead of two becoming one, it's three becoming one. And it's beautiful.

God doesn't do anything halfway. If those other intimacies are there, trust Him to supply *all* of them. And if you're sure the pending union is blessed, and you're burning

Tell Them

with passion, then elope for Pete's sake. *The wedding guests will understand.*

So you see, God found me in that hole, buried under the rubble of my house that had collapsed in the storm. Not only did He pull me out, but He built me a new house. One with a much stronger foundation than before the storm hit. He used a lot of new boards, but He salvaged some of the old ones too. He used them in the construction to remind me where I came from. To remind me there is nothing and no one who needs to stay lost in the rubble.

Now, God is telling me it's my turn to go looking for the lost.

Caroline Klug

Chapter 17
Are You Talking to Me?

Philip Yancey, a well-known American author, penned these words:

"Faith is believing in advance what will only make sense in reverse."

These words are exciting, but they can also be terrifying. They require us to have faith and imagination over what God will do *before* we can see it.

God speaks into and over our lives in so many ways. He can speak a promise to you in response to your prayers. He can plant a dream deep inside of you. He can manifest and intensify desires. If you're listening, He'll whisper guidance along the way. These whispers will require your obedience and your faith.

I went back and forth a lot on whether or not to include this chapter. I came to the conclusion that the biggest reason I was hesitant to incorporate it was because I was afraid. I was afraid what people would think if I say all of what I'm about to say, and they think it sounds ridiculous. Then I realized something important. I was writing an entire book on taking control back from the enemy, pulling out that tangled root of rejection, and walking freely in the light. Yet, I was about to omit a deeply personal chapter out of fear of rejection. For cryin' out loud, I can't even get through the blasted book without the enemy trying to get a foothold. In this case, he only had a couple of toes, so I was able to pull free. So, let's do this. Let's rip this giant, God-sized Band-Aid off.

> "Now to Him who is able to do immeasurably more than all we ask or imagine, according to His power that is at work within us, to Him be glory in the church and in Christ Jesus throughout all generations, for ever and ever! Amen." Ephesians 3:20-21

Immeasurably more. Those two words bring the Holy Spirit goosebumps to my arms. Over the years, my heart has been both tendered and electrified by what I've learned about who God is and what He's capable of, if we only believe. I'm not talking about believing I'll wake up with a six-pack replacing the squishier parts of my stomach. Although that would be great, I don't think that's quite what God had in mind when He said immeasurably more. So what *did* He mean?

I believe the secret to unleashing God's immeasurably more is quite simple. As my heart connects with His, I understand more and more how and why His power is loosed. It happens when the intentions of our hearts are unselfish and focused on His glory. It happens when we finally understand *it's not about us.* It's about winning souls for Christ and doing things that give ultimate glory to God.

Tell Them

If something good happens to us along the way, that feels great. If something we perceive as not so good happens, it might not feel so great, but God will still use it, and that makes it a win for the Kingdom.

This understanding has been both a blessing to my faith, as well as an area of intense spiritual development. I tend to have a lot of faith for the audacious.

For other people.

I believed God for big audacious things for anyone but myself. I was, for some reason, exempt. There were so many dreams pressing on my heart and building like a tornado. I say tornado, because all I seemed to expect was the destruction of my hopes and dreams. My very heart. I couldn't bear the thought of hoping for something that seemed so impossible only to get my heart shredded when it didn't happen.

But there was something else. Something even more harmful than doubt. I had a difficult time believing I was *worth* those big, audacious dreams. Surely, there were others more worthy of the vision. Surely, there were others who had lived a more obedient life and *deserved* this more than me. I didn't believe I deserved the dreams dancing in my soul, so for years, I hid them quietly away in a drawer. It was a drawer that never opened quite right, so it just seemed easier to keep it closed. There were a couple of times I was brave enough to open the drawer and show its contents to a select few.

When Kyra was very small, she sat on the floor with paper and all her crayons scattered around her. She was busy at work and I remember thinking how cute it was that she seemed so focused and engaged in whatever it was she was drawing. I say whatever because, from my vantage point, it just looked like a big blob. After a long while, she got up off the floor and ran over to me, literally squealing. She was so excited to show me what she had drawn, and held it proudly with two hands, centimeters from my face. A big blob. I pulled it away from my face a little so I could take it all in. I took it from her and looked it over carefully. That's when I saw it. I produced the biggest smile I could and told her how beautiful and amazing her horse was. She beamed. I knew my daughter's heart, and that blob magically turned into a beautiful stallion in my mind. I connected with her imagination and that encouraged her heart. A proud mama moment, for sure.

When I opened my figurative drawer to show my most precious hopes and dreams to a select few, I thought they would encourage me, like I had encouraged Kyra. There were a few, but I mostly got a pity response. You know. The kind where their somewhat encouraging words were packaged with disbelieving tone and empathetic facial expressions. I could see it all over their faces. All they saw was a blob. They thought I was nuts and they felt sorry for me for believing in my own delusions. *Bless her heart.*

Rejection followed me around like a seagull follows a kid with popcorn. Those reactions left me feeling even more uncertain, and I slammed that drawer back shut. Every once in a while, I would walk past the room the dresser was in. I would stop in the doorway and stare at it. I would even walk in and run my hand tenderly along the wood grain of the drawer and rest my hand on the handle. Then I would remember those empathetic facial expressions. I would remind myself – or, Satan would whisper – all the reasons why what I thought was God was really just a ridiculous, self-initiated dream.

Tell Them

That's not God's will for your life.

Why would God pick you?

Who are you to think you could accomplish something like that?

If someone who's known you that long doesn't think you can, neither should you.

Nonsense.

I pulled my hand away from the handle like it was a hot burner, and left the room. This time, I closed the door behind me so I couldn't even see the dresser. That's a lot like what happened during the decade of disaster. The one where I thought it was easier to run from my dream, or even get fired from it, rather than hope in it.

But God.

God brought me through that deep and long valley, and through my brokenness. He healed my heart and added to it. That's when I met and fell in love with Jim. The person I wanted to share every ounce of my heart with – including those hopes and dreams. I took his hand and I opened the door to that room. I walked him over to the dresser and I opened the drawer. Only this time, it wasn't hard to open. It slid open smoothly, like it was brand new. I'll never forget the evening. We were still dating at the time, but we both knew we were each other's forever. I should have been nervous, but I was excited. I pulled the contents of that drawer out one piece at a time, until the whole picture was set out in front of him. Like Kyra, watching my face and waiting for a reaction, I sat quietly, while he took it all in.

He smiled the most beautiful and genuine smile and spoke words so uplifting, for a moment, it felt a little like I was back having coffee with my dad while he told me I could do anything. He believed, and it made me beam like I was holding that picture of a blob. He saw it. He *saw* my stallion. And guess what? I closed that drawer again, but this time it wasn't after I put the contents back in. It was *before*. I kept them out. All the pieces. They're out where Jim and I can see them and pray over them.

I'd like to share some of them now. With you. You'll understand if I don't share all the details of them yet. But I'd like to share enough to accomplish two things. First, I don't want Fear to control me anymore. Putting it out there will help me get past that. And second, I want to be a good example and, hopefully, a help to you. I want *you* to be able to put your hopes and dreams out there.

I believe with all of my heart, there are people who will read this book who need this same encouragement. God is speaking something to your heart, but you're afraid to talk about it because it's just, well... *too* big. But God has been teaching me, the bigger the dream, the more glory for God.

There are always going to be people who doubt or even mock your dreams. Satan will send the naysayers your way in an attempt to discourage and derail you. Speaking from experience, don't be surprised if he even uses those closest to you to accomplish that task. It's more painful and effective that way. Don't let the noise in. Pray for discernment and help. After all, if your Father, the King of kings, gave you a dream, don't you think He's fully planning on being an integral part of the execution?

Tell Them

I can't help but wonder if the disconnect that was happening in my own brain with regard to my dreams might be happening in your brain. I felt certain those dreams of mine were God-given, but I lacked the confidence to expect God to execute them. Do you see how those two things are in direct conflict with each other? It's like telling your kid they should enjoy a day at the public pool, but they stay in their room because they don't want to ask you for a ride. *Didn't I just tell you I think you should go? Don't you think I'd be happy to help you get there, whether I drive you or find you another ride?* Generally speaking, people who are invested in you want to help. And God is our ultimate Investor. Not only does He want to help you, He's the One who asked, so He *expects* to help you.

Chosen One, go ahead and dream your audacious dreams. Muse and marvel in them. You may not be entirely capable or equipped. But God is. You have the God of the universe who has hung every star in its place, every planet on its axis, and drawn the boundaries of the earth and seas. He holds the world in His hands, and your dream is but a drop of water in an ocean of His glory. It's okay that you can't do it alone. *You were never meant to.*

So why couldn't I believe God would take me from my living room coffee table with an audience of One to an arena with an audience of thousands? Why couldn't I believe God would allow my books to be bestsellers and bless millions of hearts? Why couldn't I believe God would put me in a position to someday start a ministry to help make *other* people's audacious God dreams a reality?

Caroline Klug

Whoa. I just told you a lot in those three sentences. If you're closing the book now and walking away, I kind of understand. I mean, I only have like one hundred Instagram followers as I write this. But that's the funny thing about God.

> "Brothers and sisters, think of what you were when you were called. Not many of you were wise by human standards; not many were influential; not many were of noble birth. But God chose the foolish things of the world to shame the wise; God chose the weak things of the world to shame the strong. God chose the lowly things of this world and the despised things – and the things that are not – to nullify the things that are, so that no one may boast before Him." 1 Corinthians 1:26-29

God doesn't draft for His team like the NBA. He doesn't always pick the star college athlete with a proven track record. He doesn't always pick the fastest or strongest. And in my case, He certainly didn't pick the tallest. God's capabilities are so far beyond our own. Even the best and brightest need Him to accomplish those God-sized tasks. Throw a short wimpy kid onto the court, and now it's game on for God's glory. The bigger the challenge and the higher the odds *against* the team, the more opportunity for God to pull off an incredible win.

I think that's why Jesus decided to watch a few more episodes of *This is Us* before He went to raise Lazarus from the dead. In their culture, they believed the spirit stayed with the body up to three days, and departed on the fourth. By waiting until day four, all the odds were stacked against Jesus.

Tell Them

There would be no justification for Lazarus walking out of that grave, other than the supernatural power of God.

It has taken me years to talk out loud about the dreams God has planted in my heart. And it's really only been this past year where I've made a solid decision to punch Doubt in the face and just keep taking one step at a time. Even if some days it feels like I'm walking through wet concrete. Even writing this book sometimes makes me scratch my head. *Will anyone read it? Will anyone even care? Who is Caroline Klug?*

My root of rejection over the decades had conditioned me to believe that my being called was nothing more than a fantasy. It was an unattainable goal because people would *always* reject me. And nobody reads or listens to rejected human beings. Like a fad diet, I tried so many approaches through the years to getting rid of that root of rejection. Failed attempt after failed attempt usually left me sad and binge eating, and heavier than I was before I started. So what changed?

Everything, once I made the decision to act as though it *would* happen.

The day I started to actually *do* something and take the steps toward that dream, in spite of my fears, *everything* changed. The call on my life was burning hot like a magnesium fire, and I quite literally couldn't take it anymore. The spiritual restlessness I felt was unparallel to anything I've ever felt before. I had had enough. God gave me the work ethic of a bee and the drive to match it. *What was I doing sitting around feeling sorry for myself? Get up and put that drive into action. DO something. Anything.* So I started. I had a full-time job, so I spent every weekend writing my first book. And equally important, I started *telling* people I was writing a book. I even contracted with a company to build my author website, which was about as forward believing as I had ever been.

I didn't wait until I stopped feeling afraid. I just keep taking steps in spite of it.

Let's talk for a second about what led me to this feeling of being called. I told you the story of how God spoke to me on my living room sofa regarding writing for Him. What I'm about to share with you is precious and deeply personal, and I'm going to cup both my hands around it as I carefully hand it over to you to look at. I trust you.

> "During the night the mystery was revealed to Daniel in a vision. Then Daniel praised the God of heaven." Daniel 2:19

Earlier in my life, had someone talked about visions from God, I probably would have raised both my eyebrows, blinked a few times, and then walked away scratching them off my voluntary interaction list. For as touchy-feely as I can be, I'm pretty logical through and through, and visions were just not something that seemed probable in our days. Maybe in the Old Testament days, sure. But not now.

> "'In the last days,' God says, 'I will pour out My Spirit on all people. Your sons and daughters will prophesy, your young men will see visions, your old men will dream dreams.'" Acts 2:17

Three times. Three times I have been fully awake, minding my own business, when a picture of something so clear has entered my mind that it seems to transport me for

Tell Them

a second. It's not like watching it on television. It's like seeing it out of your own eyes. I'll share the most recent one, which felt like a beautiful and undeserved gift after I took a big step of faith that we'll talk about in the next chapter.

I was at the fitness center on a treadmill, between interval runs and walking at a brisk pace. My focus was on a news program on the television ahead of me when it happened. For a split second, I wasn't walking on the treadmill anymore. I was walking briskly from backstage onto the main stage. The mainstage of a giant arena. Performance lights were on as upbeat music was being played. Through my own eyes, I saw and felt my hand go up and give an energetic wave as I greeted what must have been seven or eight thousand people all clapping. Then it stopped. I was back on the treadmill. Just like that. I remember jumping onto the stationary sides of the treadmill to get off the moving belt, standing there for a few minutes trying to process what just happened.

It was significant for two reasons. The first is obvious. It felt like God giving me a glimpse of what was coming. I have no idea how or when. *Because one hundred Instagram followers.* But that's what it felt like. The second reason it was significant was because there was a message delivered to my heart in that instant. A beautiful reassurance. That moment took a nuclear bomb and set it off at the epicenter of my root of rejection. God told me those people were there of their own free will because they loved and accepted me. Because *He* loved and accepted me, and trusted me to share His message with them.

I understand if you're skeptical. I was too. All I can tell you is, it's like the difference between seeing a fire and feeling the heat of it on your arm. You can't rationalize the

208

Caroline Klug

fire away when you can feel it heating up your skin. But I get it. You might be raising your eyebrows, blinking a few times, and scratching me off the list. I realize how crazy this sounds. But I stand my ground, and I will always stand my ground in stating this was real. I felt the heat of the fire over every part of me, I inhaled the smoke in my lungs, I smelled the burning wood, I heard the crackling, and I could taste the bitterness of the smoke. Every one of my senses experienced what would otherwise be impossible to experience as I walked on that treadmill. Now, I just keep taking steps forward, in spite of my fear, and trusting in His timing.

It might be entirely possible that I now feel more frightened for people to read this chapter more so than any other. So I guess it's important I keep it in here. I can't allow Satan to cause me worry about what other people think, and force me to put my dreams back in that drawer. I need to hang my stallion on the refrigerator. Right next to my favorite *Far Side* cartoon magnet of a guy headfirst in a moving box with the caption, "There, in the box marked miscellaneous, Stewart finally found himself."

I'm fully aware some might think I've lost my mind for sharing all this, but there is at least one person out there who needs to know they are not alone. If you've ever experienced anything like this, you're *not* crazy. You're receiving a beautiful gift from God, packaged with love, and delivered via the Holy Spirit Express. Don't dismiss it. Marvel in it and dream your dreams. I know it's scary, and there is risk in putting belief in and working toward something you can't yet touch. But I think this is the heart of what separates those willing to be open to the promptings

Tell Them

and those who are too close-minded about what God can do.

I'm no exception. For a long time, I had one foot in Belief's yard and one in Doubt's. I was lukewarm, riding the fence. Riding the fence hurts your butt a lot. You can't do it for very long. I even tried getting one of those gel seats to affix to the top of the fence, but it wouldn't stay on. And every time the seat fell off, I seemed to fall into the wrong side of Doubt's yard. It was muddy and cold. I'd get back up and try to ride it out.

After a while, you've got to pick a side. I needed a lot of work and growth in this area, but after that last delivery from the Holy Spirit Express, I threw my leg over and jumped into Belief's yard. That doesn't mean Doubt doesn't mock me from the other side now and then. It just means I'm much more equipped to fight him off, because I'm standing on level ground.

As long as I'm being transparent about things I need to stop doing, I also need to stop using my shampoo and conditioner sparingly. I went to Target and bought two of those giant bottles of Nexxus shampoo and conditioner. The ones with the pumps. *I love the pumps.* They are each almost thirty-four ounces. On the front of the bottles, each one says, "New York Salon Care." For all you aspiring *New York Times* bestselling authors out there, you know the pitter patter your heart makes when you see the words *New York*. It's the epicenter of all things publishing. If you were to make a heat map of major publishing houses and literary agents across the United States, it would look like you dropped a glass bottle of ketchup. Where the bottle smashes on the floor would be New York City, and all the little splatters everywhere else would be the rest of the country.

Caroline Klug

When I first bought my shampoo bottles (which may or may not be because they had the words New York on them), I remember wondering where things might be with my books by the time those bottles were empty. You see, God had spoken something pretty specific to my heart. Every morning as I pumped a palm full of shampoo and conditioner, I would muse over what God might be doing at that moment to fulfill what He spoke. What things could be happening at the very moment I was lathering up?

Instead of leaving it at some innocent dreaming, I got it in my funny little mind that by the time I had drained those two giant tubs of hair cleanser and conditioner, God would make good on that promise. *I had just set God's timeline.* Pretty soon, those giant bottles were only half full, and I started to get nervous. I thought I'd help God out a little. *Because I'm helpful like that.* I started using *half* the amount of shampoo and conditioner than I normally use. You know, stretch it out a little and give Him a little more time.

[Facepalm] I know.

Do you see what I did there? I let Belief and Doubt comingle. I left them unsupervised and they had a baby. A really ugly one. Letting Belief and Doubt comingle is like that Scripture about combining salt water and fresh water (James 3:9-12). Once you combine them, you'll always just have salt water. And once you combine Belief and Doubt, you'll always just have Doubt.

I'm embarrassed to admit all this, but as of this morning I'm back to using the full-quantity pump, as directed for healthy, shiny hair. I can't help God with His timing. I can't manufacture due-by dates for Him because I am impatient. I might go through ten more sets of those gigantic bottles before I even see a hint of what He spoke, and I need to trust and be okay with that.

Trust. That's a big word here, folks. It implies understanding of who God is. It implies belief in who *you* are to God. It implies confidence in a plan you are utterly incapable of fully comprehending until He's ready to make it all known. It's one, big dish of unknown flavored ice cream with a bunch of I'm not sure sprinkled over the top. But that's okay. Because *He* knows. And that's all that matters. We just have to keep taking one step at a time.

Another confession. Sometimes, out of nowhere, I find myself answering pretend interview questions. Silly, I know. It's not like I think to myself, *hey, I'm going to pretend I'm being interviewed and answer questions*. A question will just pop into my mind, and before I know it, I'm sitting with the news hosts sharing my answer. I don't know how God will take me from talking into a picture mirror to answering questions on the curvy couch, but the key to getting there is believing He *can*.

A word of advice. Once you're solidly centered on the side of belief, be prepared to do what God asks of you. Anything. And guaranteed, it will get uncomfortable. Faith isn't a passive word. It's anything but. I love the way Yancey describes it in the quote at the beginning of this chapter as "believing in advance." Sometimes faith is all about praying and expecting. I consider both to be comfortable actions. But sometimes, God requires more of us, and asks us to do something I would call an uncomfortable action. This is where the rubber meets the road, as they say. And now that I was solidly on the side of belief, God made a *very* uncomfortable request of me.

Caroline Klug

Chapter 18

And Then I Published a Book...

I knew the feeling. The one that starts deep down in the pit of my stomach and stirs my insides the way Nutri-Bullet stirs my breakfast shake. God was making Himself very clear, and there was no ignoring it. It felt like a ball of impossible rolled in a lot of crazy. It didn't make any sense. I had no agent knocking at my door. I didn't even have a published book yet. Even if I did, in the literary world, I was dirt. No one knew who I was. People with no agent, no published book, and no platform do *not* quit their jobs. But that's exactly what He was asking me to do. I could *feel* it. I could even feel Him saying *now*.

Now? To say I was terrified is an understatement. By all former laws of Caroline's universe, I should have thrown myself down and pressed my body into the floor like a 2-year-old who didn't want to be picked up.

But I didn't.

"The gatekeeper opens the gate for him, and the sheep listen to his voice. He calls his own sheep by name and leads them out. When he has brought out all his own, he goes on ahead of them, and his sheep follow him because they know his voice." John 10:3-4

I knew my Father's voice, but I had spent a lifetime failing to believe Him over what I could see and touch. There were so many times I had let Fear suffocate my obedience. Regret painted the memories of too many of my decisions, and I wanted to draw a new picture. I felt like God was gifting me with an opportunity to step out and do something crazy. I don't know how to explain it other than to tell you I *knew* in my spirit God was asking me to do something crazy so *He* could do something crazy. He wanted me to step out in faith when it made absolutely no earthly sense to do so. He wanted me to show Him I trusted Him more than anything I could see.

Let me layer on to this. My company had recently been acquired by a large competitor, and we were only a few months away from formalizing the purchase. I had acquired multiple years of company stock, which would all vest at five times the new company stock price on the day the acquisition finalized. I also received a cash retention bonus, which would also pay out that same day. If I left the company even a day before it finalized, I would lose all of that. Now, in addition to walking away from my cozy salary and annual bonuses, I would leave a serious amount of cash on the table. Logic screamed that I should just stay a few more months, collect my stock and bonuses, and *then* put my notice in.

But God.

Tell Them

Those two simple words have the power to change the trajectory of my thinking. I'm sad to say they didn't always, but happy to say they do now.

So many times in the past I had heard Him whisper something, and so many times I let Doubt get in the way. Something pressed on my spirit with inhuman force, and I knew this was a make or break decision – personal and spiritual. I wanted to show God I would listen. I wanted to show Him I *loved* Him.

> "Whoever has My commands and keeps them is the one who loves Me. The one who loves Me will be loved by My Father, and I too will love them and show Myself to them." John 14:21

After all the ridiculous and copious amounts of love and mercy God had drowned me in, I wanted so badly to show Him I was a different person than before. I was a transformed human being with a grateful heart, willing and able to do whatever He asked of me. *What? You want me to go deep sea diving with bull sharks? What's that? You want me to pin chunks of chum to my wetsuit? Sure, okay. Let's do it up.*

As much as I wanted to show Him my love and gratitude, there was a motivation even more compelling. Something even more *exciting*. Like this verse says, I wanted Jesus to show Himself to me. I know that might sound strange, but I knew in my heart if I obeyed and gave this whole thing over to Him, I would see something incredible. Something that could only be credited to the work of God's hands.

Caroline Klug

You will never see God do the impossible until you give Him your impossibilities. Trust Him. He will never give you back less than what you give to Him.

We interrupt this book to bring you a test from the Heavenly Broadcast System... we repeat, this is only a test...

I wanted to pass this test with flying colors. I was there. I was terrified, but I was there. I wanted to run headlong into the unknown because I knew the character of the One who would run in before me and light the way. Now I had to have this conversation with Jim. Would he think I've completely lost my mind? Would he wonder if this logical woman he married fell out of the stupid tree and hit every branch on the way down? It would not be an easy conversation to have. *Hey, let's cut our income in half without any promise of ever making money at this. You in?* Although Fear did a few laps in my mind, just like knowing the character of my God, I knew the character of my husband. So we sat down and began to talk. There was no dancing around or up to this one, so I just dropped that turd on the table like a hot bomb. Thankfully, he didn't react the way he would had it actually *been* a turd, but we did have a serious conversation about it.

I'm going to tangent and stand up on my soap box for a minute. Because if you've made it this far, I'm hoping that means you're open minded to it.

"Do not be yoked together with unbelievers. For what do righteousness and wickedness have in common? Or what fellowship can light have with darkness? What harmony is there between Christ and Belial? Or what does a believer have in common with an unbeliever?" 2 Corinthians 6:14-15

God instructs us to avoid relationships where we are not equally yoked. This simply means you're not on the same page with something foundational. If you're dating someone who isn't a believer, don't be fooled into thinking it's a simple difference of opinion. God knew what He was doing when He gave us this instruction. He knows the damage it can cause. If you are a believer, and you're dating or considering entering into a marriage relationship with someone who isn't a believer, pray, think long and hard, and then pray some more. This foundational difference can have long-term negative impacts on both your lives and the lives of your someday children. We are imperfect beings and highly susceptible to error in judgement. Without God, we base decisions off only what we can see and feel. If we can't count on our significant others to partner with us to listen and rely on wisdom from God through the promptings of the Holy Spirit, then we are bound to flail and eventually fail.

If Jim and I were not equally yoked, this conversation would have gone much differently than it did. But because he is a man of God, and because of his love for me, his respect for me, and his trust in my own faith, he agreed to partner with me in prayer over this and take it seriously.

If you're a believer, you are going to be in situations where God might whisper something to you the world thinks is crazy. If you don't have a partner willing to go there with you in prayer and faith, it could literally alter the course of your life and send you in the opposite direction of whatever amazing thing God wants to do to or through you. Soap box thrown into the fire and burned.

I decided to do another forty-day fast. As I mentioned earlier, I had done it once before in my life, and I knew it would be difficult, but rewarding. And I desperately wanted to hear confirmation from God. Not just for myself, but unified confirmation between Jim and myself. I'll skip all the gory broccoli and tofu details, and simply say, God is good. Before that fast was up, God had spoken to both of us and we had our path confirmed.

Let me balance this with a bit of wisdom. I'm not suggesting you be reckless and take steps that are haphazard and not in alignment with what the Holy Spirit is speaking into your life.

God won't bless what He didn't set in motion.

If you know His Word and you know Him, you will know His voice. If it's His voice, and you know the promptings align with Scripture and who you know God to be, then, by all means, pursue it with reckless abandon.

When I handed in my resignation, words could not express the joy I felt in doing something for God that others might see as irrational. You see, I knew it was God asking and for that reason, I knew Jim and I could have expectant hearts. I can't wait to see what He does with the time I'm able to commit to Him.

If God is whispering something to you, I hope this brings encouragement to your heart. Step out in faith to do whatever He's asking you to do. One day, you'll be able to watch things in reverse and, what might not have made sense today will make perfect sense in His timing.

Tell Them

Spiritual giant. That's what I felt like after obeying a request that took a serious set of you-know-what to obey. For one of the first times in my adult life I felt like I completely had my crap together. Confidence-wise, I was at Rockstar status. Not arrogant, just confident in Christ. I get that I didn't quit my job and move to Rwanda to live in a tent and feed hungry babies, but this was as crazy as my risk-averse self had ever been, and it felt *great*. I didn't care what anyone thought, and *that* felt great too.

Then I published my first book.

There are three ways you can publish a book. You can self-publish, which means you have no backing from any of the big publishing houses, and you do all the work yourself. Including being a marketing department of one. Another option is to hire the services of a company to do all the work for you, but you still have no backing from any of the big publishers. Lastly and most traditionally, you can seek representation from a literary agent, whose job is to get you bragging rights in the form of a contract with one of the big publishing houses.

Getting a contract with a publishing company sounded sexy. It also sounded like a stock room full of human validation, and I started hearing Pavlov's bell ringing again. In my mind, getting picked up would validate this crazy decision to quit my job and put all the haters in their place. *Can you smell all the wrong intent wafting off the page?* Despite the mild guilt I felt over my intentions, I pushed forward and started the query process with my *Stolen* manuscript. That's where you submit information about yourself and your manuscript to agents within your genre, and age a few decades before you hear back from them. No joke. Every agent has their own specific query requirements, many say you can't query more than one agent at a firm at the same time, and most tell you if you haven't heard anything back within three months, to assume it's a no and lick your wounds. *Three months? I have to sit on my manuscript for three months before I can try again with someone else?*

Patience is not exactly one of my better attributes. Nevertheless, I was cautiously optimistic and spent a ridiculous amount of time researching agents and working on query requirements. In total, I sent out queries to twenty-six agents. Just for giggles, I'll tell you, to this day, I received communication back from five of them, and was ghosted by the rest. In hindsight, what I felt God saying was right on.

God was telling me to forget about the human validation and move forward with self-publishing. All He kept saying to me was,

"Just keep writing."

In true conversation form, I could *feel* part of what He was saying was that He didn't want me spending all that time on the query process. He just wanted me writing. So that's what I did.

Once again, I was happy to be obeying Him, but it wasn't without hits to my tender underbelly of rejection. I started out feeling slightly embarrassed telling people I was self-publishing, worried they would assume I wasn't good enough to grab an agent's attention. Again, I was caring what people thought over what God thought. Maybe all God cared about was getting my work out there for someone, and it really wasn't about *me*.

When we make things about us, we miss the forest for the trees. We miss the bigger and broader picture of what God may be trying to accomplish because our sites are set too narrow.

I wish I would have been smart enough to look at the whole forest right away rather than barrel forward and smash face first into one of the trees. I have to admit, for as much progress as I had made over the years on my root of rejection, this whole publishing a book thing ripped open a lot of old wounds. For the better portion of the month before the book went live, I was kind of a hot mess.

The book was done and ready, and the countdown to publication was on. I had been pounding the pavement on marketing and there were pre-orders coming in. There was no turning back. People were going to read *my book*. I was excited, but I was also terrified. I felt the book was good, and received great reviews from early readers I didn't know personally. If a stranger could tell me it was really good, surely those close to me would like it too.

Then it happened. I knew it was inevitable, but I wasn't prepared for it. My first hater. Only a handful of days before my book launched, two people close to me told me they didn't like the book. Not only did they not like it, but they stopped reading it. *They hated it so much they couldn't finish it?*

I was devastated. Completely and utterly devastated. *Isn't it the people who know you best who say it like it is? Doesn't that mean what they think is always true?* My book

Caroline Klug

went live in three days. It was locked for processing, so I couldn't make changes even if I wanted to. There was no time to second-guess myself, or the book. There was no time for any last-minute edits. There was no time for anything but bawling my eyes out. Which is exactly what I did. It didn't matter that an entire advance reader group told me how fantastic they thought it was. It didn't even matter that I received amazing feedback from *other* people who were really close to me. The only thing that replayed over and over in my head was the not-so-amazing feedback from two people.

Isn't it just like Satan to use the hurts of your past to mess with you during a most vulnerable moment, and trick you into prioritizing hurt over happiness?

I knew going into this there would be people who wouldn't connect with the book. I can't expect every person on the face of the earth to like my books. That sure would be great, but it's just not reality. There are plenty of *New York Times* Best Sellers out there that I couldn't finish because I just couldn't connect with it. I fully expected to get some negative reviews. However, what happened next, I didn't fully expect.

I learned pretty quickly how important book reviews are. In fact, I feel so guilty for all the books I've read without leaving a review, which I hope to remedy over time. As a new author, it's extremely important. It's one of the best tools available for readers, to help them trust unknown authors. Even when I see a new book out by someone I know and love, I *still* check the reader reviews. So I did what any new and unknown author would do, and I asked the

Tell Them

people who had read the book early to please leave a review. Outside of the unknown group of advance readers, I had given it to several others who were close to me. I had put *everything* on the line to do this, and crossed my fingers that the people close to me would support me by leaving a review.

There was someone in my life I had been close to for a very long time. They were one of the people who received an early copy of my book. I will not soon forget how I felt getting an email from them, telling me they couldn't in any good conscience leave a review on my book because they felt leaving a positive review would smear their reputation as a literary person. I was so hurt. This person had never really been along for my dream ride, which hurt in and of itself, so this left me feeling down for a long time.

I'd be lying if I said I was totally fine with it now. I still feel hurt, but I'm not upset about the lack of review. I had prayed a long time ago that God would grow my readers organically. I wanted everyone to be real and not just a padded number. The reviews did start coming in slowly from people who I knew read and honestly loved the book. Now, I feel good about that, but at the time, the response from that one person only cemented the rejection I was struggling with.

And why does everyone want to ask you how many copies you've sold? *Why, 32,000... give or take a few hundred.* No, not really. But that's what I wanted to say. I had no idea if the numbers I was seeing were good or bad. Or ugly, for that matter. Besides, isn't that like me asking someone what their gross income was last year?

Regardless, the book sold copies, and all seemed well. I started getting reviews in on Amazon and Goodreads, and with the exception of one four-star, they were all five-star and the comments were overwhelmingly positive. People were calling *Stolen* a two-sitter, meaning it was so exciting, that you read it in only two sittings. I had shaken off the naysayers, and was focusing on all the good stuff coming in.

Things were going extremely well and my book signing launch was a few days away. I wanted to look good for that, so I scheduled a haircut for the day before the signing. Something in me thought it would be a great idea to get a little edgy. *Because authors are edgy, right?* So I decided to get a pixie cut. My hair had already been on the shorter side, but I took that to a new level. I was going for chic and classy. It would be great. And then I looked in the mirror.

Sweet baby Jesus. I would have gladly traded it in for the fifth grade Snuffleupagus look. At least that I could pull back. You can't hide hair you don't have. It wasn't my hair stylist's fault – she nailed the picture I gave her. It was my bad judgement in thinking it would look good on me. It was as if Miley Cyrus' 2014 pixie cut and *Ancient Aliens'* Giorgio Tsoukalos's coif had a baby. It was not good. My only option from there was to go all late 80s Sinead O'Connor. Just no. I dealt with it, but not well. My small-town train to Rejection Central just morphed into the Japanese high-speed bullet train. I hated the way I looked, and that made it hard for me to feel secure. I wore big earrings and a lot of makeup so I wouldn't look like my brother.

The book signing went fine, and there was a good turnout, which helped bolster my confidence a little. Except for that one book I signed where I wrote something stupid and spelled a word wrong. (I thought about that for weeks.)

Tell Them

I had several other book signings scheduled over the following two weeks.

Right after my first signing, I came to learn I had done it all wrong. I happened upon a YouTube video of Rachel Hollis signing books. That's when I realized I should be using a cool sharpie marker and not just a boring pen. On my way to my second signing, I stopped at the local Office Max and acquired a fantastic set of metallic sharpies, which promoted the fact that they didn't bleed through paper. *Perfect.* Now I could sign books like I knew what I was doing. *My signature in red metallic would be worth millions someday.*

I got to the book store and set up at the little table they provided, and set the red metallic sharpie on the table directly in front of me. I was ready. The event started, and there were only two people. Me and the store owner. I played it cool and reached for a book to read until all my adoring fans showed up. I'm sure they were just grabbing a coffee at Starbucks next door in case the line for my book was long.

The next hour ticked by excruciatingly slowly. I read my book, ate the Hershey's Kisses in my candy bowl, and tried to avoid eye contact with the lady looking forlornly at me from behind the front counter. *What? Why are you looking at me like that? I'm totally fine. I have friends.*

That cool red metallic sharpie I was so excited to use never found its way out from under the cap. Not one person showed up. It was difficult not to re-evaluate my life in those excruciating hours. *My God, what have I done? What if I never sell another book?*

What if?

Girl, asking *what if* is about as useful as a blown-out flip flop in a public shower. Unless you can use it responsibly to daydream about fabulous possibilities, that question isn't going to work the way you need it to, and it's only going to leave you exposed to thoughts that can hurt you. You can't move backward. You can only move forward.

After I got home from that morale-killing book signing, ate ice cream, and moped around for a few hours, I had a mature moment of clarity. Yes, eating ice cream every time I felt sorry for myself would make me fat. However, the better clarity was remembering *it wasn't about me* and recognizing the attack for what it was.

> "It is for freedom that Christ has set us free. Stand firm, then, and do not let yourselves be burdened again by a yoke of slavery." Galatians 5:1

Rejection was my yoke of slavery. I knew it and Satan knew it. It should be no surprise that all these little things that were happening were designed to rip open wounds and leave me spiritually sick and unable to do what God called me to do. *And I was letting it happen.* Paul may have had the road to Damascus, but I had that quiet afternoon on my living room sofa, staring into an empty ice cream bowl. That's when I decided to do a new fast. Not from food. From book statistics. Prior to this moment, it was an early morning routine to check all of my book statistics.

How many books did I sell the prior day?

How many pages of my book got read on Kindle Unlimited?

Tell Them

How many paperbacks got ordered through the book store distributor?

Did I get any new reviews and what were they?

Did anyone new follow me on Goodreads?

Was anyone new reading my book or adding it to their shelf?

Seriously. This is what I did every morning. No more. I wasn't going to be a slave to what other people were doing or saying. So I fasted from all of it for two weeks, and it was the best thing I could have done. It was exciting to look at it again once I was done with my fast, but it helped to put things into perspective for me. I can't allow things like that to define success for me. If I'm doing what God has asked me to do, then I need to stop worrying so much and leave the rest of it up to Him. I do still look at those things, but I'm not a slave to them.

What I did right: I expected naysayers. I expected some poor reviews from people who just couldn't or wouldn't connect with my book.

What I did wrong: once those naysayers came forth, I didn't take them in context with the others, or look at their comments for what they were – merely someone's opinion. I took them as the be-all and end-all of my self-worth as an author. I saw it as lack of the human validation I so deeply craved.

Caroline Klug

My bowl of melted, Damascus-flavored ice cream was screaming for me to wake up and realize this whole thing was an opportunity for me to grow spiritually and pass some tests I had been repeatedly failing throughout my entire life. What happens when you fail a test? You have to take it again. And again. And again. If I was going to get off this miserable merry-go-round, I had to take this seriously and figure out how to handle things differently. It was time to pull a serious all-nighter. Stock up on the Keurig pods and almond milk. This girl is rolling up her sleeves.

Chapter 19
Aliens Are Real

After my beautifully painful moment of surrender, asking God to help me end the affair I was in, God brought a lot of amazing transformation to my heart, especially with regard to men and relationships. I was bound and determined to do things God's way. I was so confident God had this, that I decided it was a great opportunity to reveal strange facts about myself during the dating process. *Early on* in the dating process. Like, the first date, early on.

I decided a great initiation into the world of all things Caroline would be to figure out how to work into the conversation that I enjoyed watching the television show *Ancient Aliens*. Yeah, you read that right. *Ancient Aliens*. Like *The Bachelorette*, it's great entertainment. It's a fantastic mash-up of science fiction, history, theology, and comedy. Sprinkle in a random conspiracy theory or two, and you have yourself some riveting television programming. Plus, I'm secure enough in my faith to be intrigued by some of their explanations of how the things of God might be aliens. I'd like to know what people are actually buying into. *Sure, I can see how that hieroglyphic might look like an alien space ship. So you think Elijah was taken up in that alien space ship?* Riveting stuff.

When Jim and I got connected on Match.com, we had spent a week or so exchanging messages online before meeting in person. Even as we were messaging, I knew there was something special there. I knew I couldn't afford to risk being anything but myself. Things had started off great and soon, it was our fifth or sixth date. Jim had come over to my house after dinner, and was surfing through the guide on the television.

He stopped on the History Channel and said, "Ooo... *Ancient Aliens!*"

At first, I thought he was making fun of me. Then, I realized something. *I had never told him I liked that show.* I must have been so enamored with his pretty eyes that the attempt to self-sabotage the first date fell to the wayside. Once I found out he was a kindred *Ancient Alien*-watching spirit, the little hearts and birds appeared over our heads as we observed a moment of blissful and soul-melding silence. God is good. *Can I get an amen?*

I've always been intrigued by the idea of aliens. I certainly don't lose sleep over it. I mostly find the premise of it interesting, and love the awkward conversation it can create.

> *Me: Hey, did you see all the objects flying over the Fox River last night?*
>
> *Neighbor: The airplanes landing at the Airport?*
>
> *Me: No, silly. Those were scouts from the alien mother ship.*

Tell Them

Do I really believe in extraterrestrial beings? Let's just say I'm not exactly sitting out on my deck wearing a tinfoil hat, but if we ever do learn of something it would not shake my faith. It's a big universe. God can do as He chooses. On that note, did you know the Bible actually talks about aliens? No, really, it does. In order to bring this point to life, let's refresh on what an alien actually is. It simply means someone is not a citizen of the place they are living.

I got a little taste of what this feels like the first time I left the country and went to Costa Rica on a mission trip. I'll admit it was a little unsettling to step off that plane and not read English anywhere. Everything was in Spanish, and the only people speaking English were the other Americans who were on that plane with me. It gave me a new appreciation for how frightening it might be for someone foreign coming into an American airport.

My second experience with this feeling was the months (and arguably, years) leading up to quitting my twenty-year career to be a full-time author. The term I kept using was that I felt like a fish out of water. I knew I didn't belong in Corporate America. I knew there was something else I needed to be doing. It gnawed at me relentlessly. It made me restless and unsettled in my own space. I know now, that was the Holy Spirit unsettling me. Beckoning me to leave the space I was in and move somewhere completely foreign to me.

But a funny thing happened when I did that. What I first thought would feel foreign actually ended up feeling like home. More so than any other place I had been in. I was finally where God wanted me to be, and I could feel my sense of Kingdom community. The same thing happened when God called me forward out of that church pew to give my heart and life to Him. I was restless and uncomfortable in the place I was, and terrified to go forward. But once I did, I realized I was home.

> "If the world hates you, keep in mind that it hated Me first. If you belonged to the world, it would love you as its own. As it is, you do not belong to the world, but I have chosen you out of the world. That is why the world hates you." John 15:18-19

Loved One, aliens are real. *We* are the aliens. We are the ones merely visiting this earth and waiting to return to our real home, which is heaven.

That's why it can feel so uncomfortable here. We're in a constant state of hotel living. There's an unidentifiable stain on the sheets and the little bottle of lotion they leave in the bathroom doesn't smell like mountains and rain. It smells like the perfume my great aunt twice removed uses as a shower replacement. *It's not pretty.* We make do, because it's what we have. But we ache for the comforts of home. In the deepest recesses of our souls, we *know* there is something more. Something better.

All those years I felt I was different, thinking different was a bad thing. In reality, I was simply having trouble connecting with a culture that wasn't my origin. I made the mistake early on in life of believing it was all about *this* world. I got so caught up in what other people thought of me, that the idea of rejection from people held me in bondage, and caused my filter for my desires and decisions to be all out of whack. I spent years getting on and off that merry-go-round. I was sick and tired of being sick and tired.

Tell Them

In the previous chapter, I talked about a major breakthrough I had when I stopped waiting for my fear to go away before I took steps toward my call. I worked at it in spite of those feelings. I was finally pulling free of that ride. After all the work I had done to get off, for what I thought was for good, I was devastated when I allowed that fear of rejection to creep back in when I published *Stolen*. But whenever we experience a breakthrough, it's a tool we can keep in our pocket and use when needed. I kept doing what I was doing, despite my fears. I pushed past them because I believed God was bigger than what I was afraid of.

I didn't wait for my one hundred Instagram followers to turn into thousands. I just keep putting out weekly blogs, books, and social media posts, and praying they bless the following I *do* have. And every time I do get a new follower, I don't look at them like a statistic. I look at it as a responsibility and an opportunity to bring them something that will bless them and leave them better than I found them.

I take this responsibility very seriously, and I can't do any of it without God's help. I need Him as my constant companion. I pray every single day for all of my readers. And I pray every single day for God to keep illuminating the path He wants me to walk so I can reach more people and tell those people about Him.

In taking all those steps, and praying those prayers, something pivotal happened in my heart. I stopped thinking about what this means for me, and I'm now focusing on what it could mean for other people. I always knew it wasn't about me, but now I really *believe* it. That's what it took to crack the code on that root of rejection and doubt.

It took *you*.

Caroline Klug

It took praying for you and building a love connection with people whose names I didn't even know. It took understanding how I could let God use my past to positively influence *your* future.

I became an alien within my own human species. I no longer care about what happens to me in this world. I care about what happens to *you*. I care about how my actions while I'm visiting this earth impact the people I hope to share eternity with. The eternity where we all know each other's new names in Christ (Isaiah 62:2).

Don't get me wrong. Even though I've had this amazing breakthrough, I'm human, and that means I will still struggle. I will fall down. I will fail. But my feet are no longer dangling over two different sides of a fence. I'm lying on my back on the grass, in Belief's front yard and, Lord willing, that's where I'll stay. Like a recovering alcoholic, I will need to remind myself, constantly, what I'm fighting for. When I feel the press of rejection, I will call my sponsor, Jesus, for support. When I feel afraid to share a piece of my screwed-up life story or be transparent about one of my selfish and idiotic sins, I will get on my knees and I will pray for *you*. And *that* will remind me why I need to keep my life as open as this book, and let God use it. Whatever. However. Wherever. Whoever. Whyever. (I know. Not a word.)

So if you're feeling out of place, you might just be an alien. And that's okay. That's the way God designed it to work. If we got too comfortable with this hotel living, we might forget just how good it is to get somewhere without stopping on every floor along the way or plugging into a socket behind the middle of the bed frame. And if that's not enough, when we're in heaven, we won't need to walk back

Tell Them

down to the reception desk every time our room key card decides to mysteriously deactivate itself. For the third time.

Now that we're coming to terms with the realization of our origin, we should probably talk about rules while we're visiting. As with any good state, nation, or galaxy, there are always a set of rules which helps visitors maintain socially acceptable behavior while enjoying their stay. Throughout this book, I shared a lot of things I found myself in the middle of that were downright destructive. I also told you I don't do those things anymore. Part of that is, well, hot burner. But there's a very intentional part of that called boundaries. I don't want to just tell you about what I did and how I got out. I want to tell you how I *stay* out, and hope this gives you some practical ways to address any temptations you might be dealing with. If you're in a good spot, meaning, you've never entertained wrong thoughts, then I hope what I have to share can keep you in that good spot.

It's important to set boundaries for yourself, so you know when you're crossing into territory you shouldn't be in. It's also important to have an idea of when you're getting too close to that line, so you can pay attention to the warning shots. Obviously, I can't cover boundaries for every bad decision we could ever be tempted to make in life, but I can speak to a few that have helped me.

I said this earlier. When desire meets opportunity, it will either result in something wonderful if it's God-centered or something devastating if it's not.

If you're married, my first boundary is not spending time alone with someone of the opposite sex. You might find yourself justifying this by saying you have zero attraction to them and no feelings for them. Attraction develops and deepens over time and, with each opportunity, we allow it to creep past our convictions. Just because you're not initially attracted to someone doesn't mean you won't ever be. On top of that, those opportunities tend to create situations where you find yourself talking about topics that are personal, and that creates intimacy. Pretty soon, you might find yourself getting some type of satisfaction from someone who isn't your spouse, and that will start initiating all kinds of catawampus in your mind. Having others present is a great form of accountability to ensure the conversation stays appropriate and above board.

I recognize there are exceptions to this. For example, if you are a woman with a male supervisor, you might need to have a one-on-one meeting over something business-related. You can't avoid that, but you can make sure the conversation respects *topical* boundaries.

Another marital boundary – don't talk negatively about your spouse to other people. I'm not suggesting you can't seek wise counsel. What I am suggesting is that you don't make your weekly women's coffee clutch into torpedo practice and your husband is the target. Of course he's going to do things that bother or even anger you now and then. Be respectful and talk to *him* about those things, not your neighbors. Don't share things that shame or embarrass your husband openly with others. Treat him how you would want to be treated, even if he's not treating you that way back. A funny thing happens when you take the higher road. *It's attractive.* Eventually, you might find your husband following close behind. And for the love of all that's holy, try not to mother him. If you treat him like a child, it will build resentment. Pray for him, and allow him to be the

Tell Them

leader God created him to be. Let your man see you're his number one fan, and he might just turn into yours.

No matter what your relational status, don't isolate yourself from accountability. Find and connect with an accountability partner who you agree to communicate regularly with. Depending on your situation, or the things you might be struggling with, that might be weekly or it might be daily. It can be whatever you need and agree to in order to maintain active accountability. Finding this person may not happen quickly, as it sometimes takes a little time to build the right kind of rapport which cultivates this type of relationship. But once you do, make sure your accountability partner has free reign to ask you whatever they need to. If you start creating limitations on things you can and can't talk about, this might lead to areas of grey the enemy will use to tempt you. This should go without saying, but this accountability person should not be someone of the opposite sex.

Don't assume you can always figure it all out. Seek out a mentor. This individual can function much the same way as an accountability partner, but they are present in your life as a teaching influence. They are someone typically older or more experienced than yourself who can help guide and shepherd you in your personal life and spiritual walk. They don't have to have all the answers, but they should be able to help you navigate life situations using solid, biblically based wisdom.

This next one is a little more complicated, but will pay enormous dividends if you can do it. Don't allow your triggers to dictate what you do. If you know what your triggers are – those things that make you feel vulnerable to compromise – then you'll be able to see them for what they are and stop the reaction before it happens. For me, rejection was a trigger that made me susceptible to attention from unhealthy sources. For you, maybe your sin is overeating, and one of your triggers is seeing a fashion magazine with pictures of women you feel you could never look like. If you see those images, don't follow it up with a trip to the grocery store. And for what it's worth, *no one* looks like that. *It's called an air brush.*

Whether your trigger is tangible or just a negative thought, compare what you're seeing or hearing to Scripture. It's a quick way to get to the truth, and then be able to dispel the lie. If you find a Scripture that supports truth, memorize it. Memorize it and say it out loud every day. Write it on little note cards and stick it to your bathroom mirror. Or the refrigerator. Whatever you need.

On that note (pun intended), if you do struggle with body image issues, then I don't so much have boundary, as much as I have some practical advice for you. But first, a disclaimer. I realize that when people look at me, at 5'3" and 120lbs, it's hard for them to think I could have body image issues. If you're not sure I could struggle with that, go back and read the chapter about my tummy tuck. Or the one about struggling with bulimia. It's a real thing, no matter what your shape or size.

I'll apologize in advance if this sounds like a lot of preaching, but I hope you take it in the spirit it's meant. Just know, I'm preaching to myself when I say this. Unless you have some type of condition which makes your weight issue something beyond your human control, then my advice is to stop *talking* about doing the work and start *doing* the work. Nothing is ever going to change unless you take the steps to take care of yourself. You can't think yourself into shape. (My selfish hope is that by saying this to you, I am now forced to follow my own advice.)

If we're honest, most of the time when we feel disappointed in ourselves for how we look, the reality is, there is more we can do. We just choose not to, and end up feeling sorry for ourselves. Stop looking in a mirror and *wishing* you looked different and make the uncomfortable changes to *be* different. Stop drinking the soda you don't need. Stop eating fast food and pack a healthy lunch instead. You don't *need* a mocha every day. You *want* a mocha every day. But if you want to lose a few pounds and feel better, then you're going to have to make a choice. Maybe you have that mocha once a week, and only after you hit your exercise goal.

I think it's important to talk about this, because when you're not feeling your best, that can negatively influence a lot of things in your life – especially your self-image. Even if you haven't reached your goal yet, if you're *doing* the work and eating right, I guarantee you're going to feel better about yourself. It will be a major boost to your self-confidence.

There is one more boundary I'd like to talk about. It's about surrounding yourself with people who make you the best version of you. Close friendships are not only healthy, but if you happen to have two X chromosomes, then they are critical. I firmly believe women need women. I love my husband immensely, and I love having conversations with him, but there is just something to be said about getting together with other women I align with, and breaking bread with them. *With wine. And maybe some chocolate. And maybe this new thing my southern friend introduced to me called sausage balls.* We all need our tribe. There's a camaraderie there which can be very uplifting, or, if broken, very disabling.

> "As iron sharpens iron, so one person sharpens another." Proverbs 27:17

People say you are what you eat. Well, you're also going to become who you hang out with. It's inevitable. You will either be the influencer or the influenced. Either way, you have to be careful about what and who you're allowing into your heart. I take full ownership of the wrong things I have done, but I sometimes wonder if some of that would have been avoidable had I had friends at the time who were strong enough in their faith and their love for me to tell me what I was doing was wrong. I wish they would have loved me enough to tell me I was destroying my life and the lives of others. If your tribe is enabling you, then you might need a new tribe.

Likewise, I had friendships in my life with people who were the ones dancing with death. I wish *I* would have been that friend strong enough to tell *them* what they were doing was wrong. But I wasn't. I enabled them because I wanted their enablement back. For that, I am sorry, and regret those choices. But once more, you can only move forward. Since getting myself right, I know what I will continue to do if my friends find themselves in situations that require love and truth. They will always get both.

Something else that's critical about your tribe is how they leave you, and how you leave them at the end of the day. Do your conversations leave you feeling encouraged and built up? Or do they leave you feeling down or convicted? Do they make you the best version of you, or the version that needs a time out? If it's any of the latter, then you need a new tribe. You, Loved One, are worth so much more than that. You deserve people who will bring out and sharpen the wonderful parts of you, and dull and remove the not-so-wonderful parts.

Having a tribe that's tight, filled with people who I love and trust, and who I know love and trust me has been a cry of my heart for a long time. I am relational to the core, and the Labrador in me just wants to love and be loved. I was frustrated for a long time with feeling like my relationships were more of a one-way street. I was always the one doing and scheduling everything, and the minute I stopped, everything else stopped. It's like I was completely forgotten about and that just triggered that rejection even more deeply. So I started praying.

A funny thing happens when you start praying about your relationships. God has a way of answering. He has certainly done that for me, bringing several beautiful and faith-filled women into my circle. The people you allow closest to you are the people who are going to influence you for the good, bad, or ugly. For this reason, I believe God is extremely interested and invested in who we choose to call our tribe.

When Jim and I moved into our condo, I walked through every room and prayed over each and every window and doorway. I prayed our home would be one of blessing and welcomed God into that place. I prayed anyone who entered would experience comfort and His presence. But I didn't stop there. The unit next to ours was still open, so I prayed for that one too. But I found myself asking God for a friend. I know that might sound silly, but I remember it being more of a statement than a prayer.

Caroline Klug

"God, wouldn't it be cool if whoever moves in next door was someone I could connect and be friends with? Wouldn't it be so cool if she was a Christian? Wouldn't it be cool to have someone so close by that I could walk barefoot over to her place for a glass of wine, while we laugh about our day and encourage one another?"

I'm imagining, at the time, God was like, "Gee, Caroline, what a great idea."

We are made in His image, so I assume He is also capable of sarcasm. In this case, He was way ahead of me. It tenders my heart how God orchestrates and plants the desires of our heart. A few weeks later, a single woman moved in. This southern accent-speaking, surgical knife-wielding, Jesus-loving individual and I became fast friends, and I adore her. She's a surgeon, and I feel a kindred spirit to her because I've watched every season of *Grey's Anatomy*.

The message here is simple. God cares, and when you ask Him for things that will ultimately honor Him, He'll answer. Especially when those things honor the boundaries you are thoughtfully setting around yourself, so you can keep living your best life while visiting this earth.

Speaking of visiting earth, if you ever happen to see an octopus, be very nice to it. They are wicked smart. All on their own, they can figure out how to twist the top off a jar to get to what's inside of it. I'm fairly certain they're aliens.

Chapter 20
The Hail Mary

Jim is an animal lover. He has a great respect for creatures, and treats them all kindly, with limited exception. Like that time he launched one off his front porch.

When Jim and I first met, he was living in a log cabin sitting in the middle of nine acres of woods. We later termed it The Compound, as we felt it would make an excellent survival location in the event of the apocalypse – zombie, alien, or other. One evening, Jim was walking back to the house from his workshop when he heard a cat crying. As he got closer to the front porch, he could see the outline of it and its matted fur. He thought it was the neighbor's cat, so he scooped it up in his arms and cradled it like a baby. He stepped onto the porch and took a few steps closer into the porch light to get a good look at his feline friend.

Have you ever stared into the face of an angry possum, mouth agape and sharp teeth showing? Well, Jim just did. He screamed like a girl and then launched the vile creature back into the abyss from which it came.

Caroline Klug

Moral of the story? Sometimes things are not what they seem.

Every person has a story. Every person has a kaleidoscope of life experiences – good and bad – that make up who they are, how they think, and how they react. We may know how *we* would respond to certain situations, but unless we know someone's story, we can't presume to understand why they did what they did, or why they continue to do what they do. We shouldn't give people a pass for living in some type of sin, but we should approach someone first and foremost with the love of Christ, and leave the judgement part to Him. Sometimes, we need to assume we're dealing with a cat instead of a possum.
Judgement is one of the quickest ways to shut another person down. Not only is it a form of shaming, but it will completely kill any opportunity to positively influence that person. If they don't feel they can talk to you without getting shamed, then they will never open up. And that can be a loss for both of you. They may not have someone to learn from. Did you ever think that might be why God sent you across their path? Perhaps God ordained that interaction as an opportunity for *you* as much as it was for that person.
I'm not exempt from judging people. The struggle is real. It's hard sometimes not to look at someone's behavior, feel put off by it, and try to be their Holy Spirit, telling them right from wrong. Being put off by sinful behavior is okay – Jesus showed us that when He turned over the tables of the people who turned His Father's house into a flea market (John 2:13-16). What isn't okay is self-righteous indignation. Instead of trying to be their Holy Spirit, we need to first try to be their friend. Then, when that relationship is

established, and there's a foundation of trust, we can invest and sow wisdom into it. The beautiful thing about that is, even if you're the one doing the helping, through that process, you will find yourself being blessed with understanding the circumstance of another.

Like I said, I'm not exempt from the temptation to judge. I've already confessed the indiscretions of my heart while watching *The Bachelorette*. But because of everything I've been through, I do have a tendency to have a tender heart toward someone I suspect might be in trouble. I know what it feels like to be judged critically, but I also know what it feels like to be loved unconditionally. There is no comparison in terms of which will help a person more.

Love wins every time.

I was speaking at a women's retreat one weekend, and one of the women came to me after. She shared things she was struggling with that would be, by anyone's account, sinful. I could have given her a litany of reasons why she should stop doing what she's doing, but in that moment all I felt God tell me was to love her. Without saying anything, I simply hugged her. For an awkwardly long time. Until she finally hugged me back. Like, really hugged me back. Once we got past the awkwardness, there were a lot of tears from both of us. That simple act opened the door for a lot more conversations to come. She didn't feel threatened, judged, or unloved, so she opened up even more. I learned so much from that interaction, and how powerful it can be to let someone know you care in such a simple way. For the record, not everyone likes to be hugged or touched. You

Caroline Klug

should probably follow those Holy Spirit promptings so you don't get sucker punched.

With that said, I'd like to talk about who I wrote this book for, including a Hail Mary audience I have been praying for.

The first audience was myself, as a means of exhuming my bones and walking fully in the light. I can tell you, writing this book was not at all what I expected it to feel like. When I started, I felt so fearful and anxious. I thought working through this would leave me feeling unsteady and cause me to roller coaster through my emotions. I even remember asking Jim in advance for his patience because I thought working on this book might cause me to act differently for a while. It *did* cause me to act differently.

When Jim and I sold our house in Kaukauna, WI, before moving to our condo in Green Bay, WI, part of the sale agreement with the new owner was that we had to re-level our brick patio. The bricks had settled all wonky, which was driving water toward the foundation of the garage and house. Rather than hire this out, we figured we could tackle it, being the strong, able-bodied people we were. To say this was a large undertaking is an understatement.

I don't know why I'm being polite right now. I'll just say it like it is. It was horrendous. We pulled out and stacked thousands of bricks. We loaded over one ton of sand and gravel onto a cart, into the car, out of the car, and onto the patio. That's over two thousand pounds each time we transferred those materials. We then unstacked and re-laid those several thousand bricks. And we did it all in the matter of a few days. I can still remember working to get the bricks in before the approaching thunderstorm did any damage to the exposed and leveled sand and gravel. My arms were so sore and tired, I could barely pick up a single brick without wincing.

Writing this book has made me feel like that process in reverse. In the beginning, I was exhausted and barely felt able to do the work. With every bone I exhumed and wrote about, it was like moving backward through that process. It got easier and easier, I got stronger and stronger, and the work felt lighter and lighter. *I* got lighter and lighter.

You might be thinking, "That's great. You moved backward through the process and now you're back, staring at a wonky brick patio." I get where you're coming from, but I'd like to offer a different perspective. I did feel like that process moved backward, but now I don't need to put it back together. God will.

> "Unless the Lord builds the house, the builders labor in vain." Psalm 127:1a

Loved One, when you let God into the darkest parts of your life, He can help you dig up the unstable foundation so *He* can rebuild it. If God is doing the leveling and the building, you can rest assured it will be beautiful, and its foundation will be solid.

That is what I feel today, as I write these words. Solid. Level ground is a beautiful thing. What are you standing on?

The next audience was anyone who might be caught up in, or thinking about, things that would lead them down a dark path and away from God. Take it from someone who's failed the test more times than I care to admit, *it's never worth it.* I sincerely hope my transparency within these pages has helped you to see that. At a minimum, I hope it's helped you know how to identify some of the dark corners you might be headed toward, if not already sitting in.

Now that we've gotten this far, I think you're ready for some hard truth. I hope you are, because it's coming. I want you to take a deep breath and really hear me out on this next part.

If you're honest with yourself, you know what you're hanging onto isn't right. You know now and you've known from the very beginning. Whether it's an emotion, a lie from the enemy that's preventing you from healing, or even a sin fully manifested in your life, you know when you're hanging onto something that isn't of God. You know because of that stir in the pit of your stomach telling you so. If it's stirring right now as you're reading this, I beg you not to ignore it. What I'm saying was birthed from a lot of poor decisions, and a lot of regretful hindsight acknowledging what I always knew to be true but was too emotionally involved and scared to admit.

That stir isn't pain. It's a gift. It's the amazing gift of the Holy Spirit. God is loving you enough to warn you that where you're headed isn't going to end well for you. He's trying to tell you He has a better plan. The *best* plan.

Beloved, I know you might be scared. I know, because I was terrified. For years. Almost decades. For so many years I let Satan manipulate me into silence, but with that silence came agony. It was always there, that steady undercurrent of awareness of the bones buried so deep beneath my feet. Those bones kept me unsteady. I wasn't walking on level ground and even though I might not have been struggling

Tell Them

anymore with the sin that created those bones, I was always distracted by their presence.

There is a better way to live. A freer, truer, and more peaceful way. In order to get there, we need to be able to say it out loud.

> "When Jesus saw him lying there and learned that he had been in this condition for a long time, He asked him, 'Do you want to get well?'" John 5:6

Sometimes God asks us the obvious question. We say a lot of things in our heads, but it gets real when we say it out loud. God is a gentleman and He's never going to force Himself on you, but He will ask and wait for you to respond. God has every capability to help you, but you have to want it. It can't be just Him wanting it for you. It has to be of your free will.

> "'Sir,' the invalid replied, 'I have no one to help me into the pool when the water is stirred. While I am trying to get in, someone else goes down ahead of me.' Then Jesus said to him, 'Get up! Pick up your mat and walk.' At once the man was cured; he picked up his mat and walked." John 5:7-9a

Isn't it just like us to make excuses and focus on all the reasons we can't? Before I go on, I want to say something important so I'm not misunderstood. Getting on my knees and begging God to help me was just where I was at. I was being held captive and my strength was failing. That doesn't mean that's always the answer, to ask and just wait for God to show up and fix it. I remember that moment as clear as day, and my intentions had nothing to do with being lazy or half-hearted in my request. There was a genuine life and death struggle going on inside of me and that prayer was all I had in me. But sometimes the answer is obvious and only requires us to *do* the obvious – which is usually to walk away. Quite frankly, maybe it happened the way it did for me by design, because God knew my heart's cry was genuine, and needed that man to be the one to do the obvious for *his* own heart's sake.

Don't over-complicate what it means to be free. Stop overthinking and trust that if you follow God's Word, you will have the best chance for the best outcomes. Satan will lie to you and tell you your truths will keep you in prison. He's a liar. God's Word already tells us the truth will set us free (John 8:32). Try not to be narrowly focused on the loss or pain you're afraid of feeling in the moment. Instead, try focusing on the joy that will be yours once you're fully walking in the light. No hiding. No secrets. No trying to keep your story straight. Only the simple truth. Anything else is exhausting.

Coming clean on things comes with some challenges. You *will* have to deal with some initial reactions. Some will be loving and merciful and some may be harsh. You might even be the subject of a little conversation for a brief time, but as soon as something new and scandalous happens on the next episode of *The Bachelorette*, no one will even be talking about you anymore. But in all seriousness, it will pass. It always does. And you know what? His grace is sufficient to get you through (2 Corinthians 12:9), and that peace that surpasses understanding will cover you (Philippians 4:7).

The next audience is made up of those who have repented of past sin, or healed from past trauma, but still have bones buried in their yard that they are afraid of people finding. After inviting you into the ceremonial exhumation of my own bones, I'm hoping you now believe hiding them causes way more stress and pain than exposing them.

It's true that haters are going to hate, but one of Satan's lies is the exaggeration that you will have more haters than supporters. I can tell you from personal experience that it's just not true. As I sat down with people in my life – some close and some not as close – and began sharing transparently about this book and what's in it, my heart was humbled at the love and mercy shown from those individuals, including from my own daughter. *Talk about another proud mama moment.* I also think the older people are, or the more radically their hearts have been changed for Jesus, the more grace and mercy that is born out of understanding.

Which is a good segue to the explanation of that Hail Mary audience I have been praying for.

I want to acknowledge this is a hard audience. Really hard. The odds are against me with this one, but you know what they say?

> "Jesus looked at them and said, 'With man this is impossible, but with God all things are possible.'" Matthew 19:26

For those of you who have been on the other side of these wrongs, whether by my hand or someone else's, *you* are my Hail Mary audience. Forgiveness is incredibly difficult. As Christians, we are called to give it, but that doesn't always make the mess around us disappear. What I've found from personal experience, is that it does make the mess *inside* us disappear.

Caroline Klug

If you have been personally hurt by anything I've shared in this book, then, from the bottom of my heart and soul, I want you to know how very sorry I am. I am so sorry that I did things or took things that I can't undo or give back. I am so sorry that my selfishness, immaturity, insecurity, and entitlement caused you pain or, worse, loss. I know there's nothing I will ever be able to do to make it right, so my only hope and prayer is that you allow Jesus to make it right. Please forgive me. Forgive me, and allow Jesus to fix whatever I so stupidly broke.

If you've been hurt by someone else, I can't apologize for them. But regardless of whether or not that person is repentant, forgiveness is still the way to find your peace. Don't allow those individuals to steal another moment from your life. Take the control and give it over to Jesus. If you can find it in your heart to forgive, He will – immediately or over time – bring peace to your soul.

> "For our struggle is not against flesh and blood, but against the rulers, against the authorities, against the powers of this dark world and against the spiritual forces of evil in the heavenly realms." Ephesians 6:12

Our battles are not with each other. These people who hurt you – they are hurting themselves. What would happen if we could all accept a different perspective and see the sick person for what they are? *Sick*. People who hurt other people need help addressing the reasons for their behavior. I'm not suggesting you try to work with someone who is physically or sexually abusing you. You need to remove yourself from those life-threatening situations. What we should do is try a little harder to seek to understand

Tell Them

whenever possible, and try to see someone the way God sees them. Sometimes the most profound and impactful witness can be loving someone when they feel unlovable or forgiving them when they expect to be judged. Especially by the person they wronged.

> "Jesus said, 'Father, forgive them, for they do not know what they are doing.'" Luke 23:34a

This is Jesus' response as He hung, beaten and dying on the cross. He was asking His Father to forgive the people who beat Him, drove stakes into His hands and feet, and mocked Him. He was asking His Father to forgive every act of injustice that had ever been or ever will be committed. That includes the acts of injustice done by you and me. Jesus is our example in all things. Jesus forgave us first. It's our turn to forgive each other.

Which brings me to my final confession: I am a hypocrite.

I spent years judging people for the hurts they caused me, and then I fell into the same pit. I wasn't better than the men who cheated on me just because I wasn't with someone. In fact, I was worse because I knew better.

> "For I am the least of the apostles and do not even deserve to be called an apostle, because I persecuted the church of God. But by the grace of God I am what I am, and His grace to me was not without effect. No, I worked harder than all of them – yet not I, but the grace of God that was with me." 1 Corinthians 15:9-10

Caroline Klug

These are words from the Apostle Paul. Before God met him on the road to Damascus and transformed his heart, he spent his days persecuting Christ followers. He wasn't just a non-believer. He was a hater. A murderer. Jesus changed Paul's heart, but Paul always knew where he came from. He knew and never denied what he had done. But he also knew and believed he was now a slave to Christ, body, mind, and soul.

Paul went on to be one of the most significant influencers of the entire New Testament. What might have happened if no one ever forgave Paul? What might have happened if people only saw what he had done and refused to see what *God* had done *in* Him? In the spirit of healthy fantasies, I like to imagine the loved ones of Paul's murder victims came to know Christ because of the radical transformation they were firsthand witnesses to. It doesn't make the loss easier, but it shows how God can use it.

Here's a final thought with regard to people and audiences. We'll call this a BOGO (Buy One Get One) free deal. I suspect some of you may be lucky enough to have no bones in your yard, but you might struggle to understand someone who does or did. I hope the words I've shared have, at least in some small way, helped you to first seek understanding when dealing with someone who's story you may not know. And even once you do know it, to seek the path of love.

Love wins. Every time.

Tell Them

Chapter 21
Putting My Bra Back on

Years ago, I had dropped my car off at an auto garage for general maintenance, so they kindly shuttled me to work. At the end of the day, I passed through the turn styles by security, and waited in the enclosed entranceway for the shuttle to show up and take me back to my car. Something I had eaten over lunch didn't agree with me, and I was feeling really bloated. I realized in that moment I *really* had to pass gas.

For those of you who know me, hearing me do this would be as elusive as seeing Yeti in the flesh. To this day, my husband believes I neither poop nor fart. It's kind of an understanding between us. *Some things should remain a mystery.* The fact that I'm even sharing this story is probably testament to out of body experiences. I must be hovering above mine, unaware of what my fingers are typing.

So I'm leaning against the wall trying really hard to hold it in. I look around. I'm alone in the entranceway. *No one is coming.* The security guard is engrossed in something on his computer monitor. But even if he *was* looking at me, it's not like he'd be able to tell I just farted. Unless I had that

Caroline Klug

I'm farting right now look on my face. How would I know? I had never looked at myself in the mirror while farting. I couldn't take it anymore, so I threw caution to the wind. Along with something else.

At the moment of my indiscretion, someone I knew came flying around the corner and through the turn styles like a kid on the last day of school. I thought about running out the door, but she had already seen me standing there. Any attempt to flee would only incriminate me further. Besides, I told myself there's no way she's going to smell anything at the rate of speed she's moving. What happened next was like a slow-motion death scene in a teen horror flick.

Just as the woman smiled at me and grabbed the handle of the door to the entranceway, a second, involuntary fart escaped. I could feel the heat in my face, and just hoped she would maintain speed, so this horrific event would soon be over. The wall I was leaning against had an air vent level with my butt. As soon as she stepped inside, it started blowing air past me and into her. What I tried so hard to hide became front and center.

Yeah, I know.

This book has felt kind of like that moment. I told you I was going to take off my proverbial bra, but I'm pretty sure I just stood on the table and twirled it around my finger. So, sorry about that. It had to be done. It had to be said. And I'm pretty sure that's all of it. I was trying to think if there were any more dangling participles, because I don't ever want to have to go through this morbid exercise again. Outside of an isolated teen shoplifting incident and some not so isolated stupid-driver induced cussing, I believe all the

Tell Them

bones are accounted for. *I did it.* He asked me to tell you, and I did.

> "The Lord said, 'Go out and stand on the mountain in the presence of the Lord, for the Lord is about to pass by.' Then a great and powerful wind tore the mountains apart and shattered the rocks before the Lord, but the Lord was not in the wind. After the wind there was an earthquake, but the Lord was not in the earthquake. After the earthquake came a fire, but the Lord was not in the fire. And after the fire came a gentle whisper. When Elijah heard it, he pulled his cloak over his face and went out and stood at the mouth of the cave." 1 Kings 19:11-13

There's a reason the title of this book is formatted the way it is on the cover. When I heard God say, "Tell them," I wanted to encompass the emphasis behind His words. Using all lower case symbolizes the still, small voice of God. The Scripture above tells us He doesn't always come in earthquakes or storms. He comes in the still of the moment, speaking so quietly at times, that we need to lean in to hear Him. When you spend time with Him and in His Word, you are leaning in. You are listening and adjusting your radio to pick up His frequency. The letters are fat and bold to symbolize His instruction. The voice may have been still and small, but the breadth of His message was not. It will remain with me for a lifetime, and be an ever-present reminder of the importance of transparency, and the freedom that comes when you find the courage to walk in the light.

Caroline Klug

"Therefore confess your sins to each other and pray for each other so that you may be healed. The prayer of a righteous person is powerful and effective." James 5:16

My call is clear, and I desire the work of my hands to be effective. I couldn't do that as long as there were things remaining hidden. I'll bring you onboard the sailboat for a quick story, to help show you how *useless* can turn to *useful*.

The first long sail Jim and I ever took was in our first sailboat, a 30-year-old Catalina 25. We sailed from Green Bay, WI to Little Sturgeon, WI, which was only about thirty or so nautical miles. We were still learning how to sail, so maximizing hull speed wasn't really a thing for us yet. If we got up to four knots, we were pretty happy. That sail took us nine hours. I'd like to say it was magical, but I spent most of it sick to my stomach, wondering what horrible thing I had just gotten myself into by agreeing to buy this sailboat. On the sail back home, I was sick, frustrated, and I wanted to throw in the towel. I was silently deciding sailing just wouldn't be for me. I just had to get up the nerve to tell Jim, who so clearly was falling in love with it.

Moments before I was about to open my mouth and dash his dreams, Jim grabbed the line to pull out the headsail, which is the sail in front of the big mainsail. In doing so, he stepped backward and directly onto my foot. With each heave of the line, he was grinding his heel into my big toe. The only thing that seemed to come out of my mouth was a steady stream of "ow ow ow ow..." He looked at me with wide eyes and let go of the line, thinking I was somehow caught up in it, but he never took his weight off his heel, so I continued to howl, "ow ow ow ow..." That's when he looked down and finally figured out what was going on.

Tell Them

That howl was really the culmination of the irritation I was feeling over not wanting to be on that sailboat. As soon as Jim stepped off my foot, I was about to vomit my despise for the whole thing and swim home. That's when God closed my mouth and said something very clearly to me. Almost with the tone of a disciplining parent.

"You are not quitting. I'm using this to teach you both about partnership."

Talk about humbling. After all the years I prayed and begged for a true partner (my words) and now God was shushing me and explaining this was one of the ways He intended on accomplishing that. Fast forward three years, and we now laugh hysterically about that moment. What's even better, is my love for sailing caught up with his, and we both have our captains' licenses. We talk and dream all the time about our retirement boat, which will be named Gratitude, which we will use to someday sail around the world to see the wonders of God's hands. I'm so glad God blessed me with those words, and so glad Jim was patient with me. *I love your heart, Sugar Blossom.*

I told you that story just so I could talk about the difference between a rope and a line. In laymen's terms, they are one in the same. In the sailing world, it's a rope when it's hanging on the wheel at the marine store. Once it's cut and installed as something useful on the sailboat, it's then called a line. So the primary difference between a rope and a line, is one is useful and one isn't.

What will your life story be? Will it be a rope or a line? Will you stow it away where it can't be useful, or will you allow God to craft it and give it purpose? You might think some things can't be purposeful, but God says He can use *all* things (Romans 8:28). Give it to Him and let Him be the judge.

A big reason we bury bones is because we're afraid of what others will think or what we might lose if others know about what we did. The consequences of sin are very real, but so is God's forgiveness and mercy, as I hope you've gleaned from my own love story. What God is able to do with the dark and twisty parts of your life will far outweigh and overcome whatever you're afraid will happen if you walk in the light. Just like we talked about when feeling afraid of entering into something that feels spiritually alien to us, you'll be just as surprised at the supernatural transformation that happens when you give it all over.

> "Therefore, if anyone is in Christ, the new creation has come: The old has gone, the new is here!" 2 Corinthians 5:17

There's something I haven't said yet, but this feels like a good place to say it. After everything I've told you about my past and the things I've done, I want to be clear about one thing. I'm *still* the other woman, but *other* takes on quite a new meaning now. I'm not the person I used to be. Not even close. I may still have a warped sense of humor and enjoy adolescent poop stories, but the pieces of my flawed character that caused me to make those poor decisions so many years ago were left behind in the grave when Jesus called me out of it. Those pieces were my grave clothes. But not anymore. I am a new creation, clothed in love and fed with the sweet fruit of forgiveness.

Tell Them

I'm not perfect, and I'm sure I'll sin again – probably the next time someone pulls in front of me without using their blinker. But I'm no longer dying from spiritual cancer. I no longer feel hopeless. I'm alive, and as long as I stay that way, I'm going to devote my heart to helping as many people as I can to know the God I love.

When we started our time together, I said Satan will always try to manipulate you into thinking God isn't real, He's far away, He's unloving, or He's unfair. Cherished One, I hope my story has shown you a different side of Him. I hope it has opened your eyes to the God of all heaven and Earth who is loving and close to us. I pray you can feel He is as real as the air you and I both breathe. I also hope you can see He is not only fair but merciful. If we want to talk fairness, what I deserved for my actions was death and misery. Instead, He left the ninety-nine and He found me. He loved me. He healed my wounds and He gave me more than I could ever deserve in this lifetime or the other side of heaven. If that isn't a picture of a loving God, I don't know what is.

This isn't just my life story. It's my *love* story. And, Lord willing, it's far from over.

Jim and I had only been dating for a month (which was about two weeks more than I needed to know I was going to marry him), when I felt convicted that I needed to tell him about some of the dark and twisty sins of my past. A part of me knew telling him might mean I lose him, but that was all the more reason it was the right thing to do. I knew he felt the same for me, but if there was even a small chance that anything I had done in my past would spook him, then

I owed it to both of us to be upfront. I also felt it was important to establish trust. I knew this relationship was of God, and I wanted to give it the respect it deserved.

When God told me to tell all of you, one of the reasons was the same as why I had to tell Jim. So, here it is. I've taken you through who I was, what I had done, and who I am today. I can't promise to be perfect, but I can promise you authenticity, and the death of my pride for the sake of the Kingdom. If I make a mistake, I'll own up to it. If I say something I shouldn't, I'll apologize. What I'll never apologize for is my call to write and speak and minister to as many hearts as Christ will allow me the privilege to serve. If yours could be one of them, I'll do my best to earn and keep your trust. This book is the first big step to that.

I told you in the beginning, this book isn't just for me. It's for you, too. You, Loved One, have a story to tell. Good, bad, or ugly, it makes no difference. God can use it all, no matter what it is. I understand how tempting it is to hide things. But it's not about us.

Your story isn't just about what happens to you. It's about how you let God use the ugliest parts of your past to help others with their future.

Sometimes it's all about perspective. Think about when Jesus died on the cross. The Apostles must have felt hopeless as they tried to process the events of that dark afternoon. Walking away from Golgotha was probably more difficult than walking to it. They were grieving what they thought was the permanent death of their Master and close friend. Surely, they were confused and even questioned the validity of what they had been a part of. They didn't understand the significance Jesus' crucifixion held for the future of all of mankind and eternity. All they felt was loss.

What the Apostles saw as horrible, heaven saw as the catalyst for the hope and salvation of mankind. As humans, we struggle all the time with our definitions of good and bad. We see bad things happen and get angry when sometimes, those things are a catalyst for the better things God is doing. I'm in no way diminishing the pain that hard circumstances can force us to face. Jesus wrote the book on that. The physical, mental, and emotional torture He suffered during crucifixion was nothing short of horrific. But He did it for the joy set before Him – for us.

Because of Jesus' sacrifice, no matter who you are and no matter what you've done, you are invited to come forth to the altar. To the Throne Room. To the center of the Holy of Holies. To stand as you are within the very presence of God Himself.

What an honor and privilege we have to be invited into the presence of our loving God.

I can tell you, now that I've fully accepted the gift of forgiveness, I genuinely feel like that new creation. I've been "saved" for a long time, but I've never felt this whole. I feel released to do the work He's called me to do, and I'm no longer afraid of the dark.

"Then you will know the truth, and the truth will set you free." John 8:32

I'm free now. Satan no longer has a hold on me. There is nothing left in the dark he can hurt me with. It's in the light. Where it should be. Where it will stay. If your story looks even remotely like mine, then you must be exhausted. You might think you don't have the energy to do any digging. Let me assure you, the rest and reward for that work will far outweigh the task.

> "Whoever conceals their sins does not prosper, but the one who confesses and renounces them finds mercy." Proverbs 28:13

I'm sure you've heard the saying that says the whole is stronger than the sum of its parts. This is true for many things, like the church. But what if that also applies to all the pieces and parts of your life? Even the ones you'd like to return with a receipt. When all the pieces of your story come together, it can produce something more powerful than all the individual pieces that left you feeling shattered.

Be brave, and don't hide anymore. Your shattered glass can reflect light. Like an SOS signal into the darkness, so is your story to someone who needs to hear it. It could be the very catalyst that helps someone heal from their own shame and guilt.

God is our Father. If you have kids, think about what lengths you would go to see your child happy, healthy, and full of joy. Now multiply that by a bazillion. He loved me even when I turned my back on Him, even *after* I had full knowledge of His love and faithfulness and the reality of His presence. I knew God and still did these things, and He *still* loved me back into His arms. My love letter can be your love letter, and yours can be a billion other people's.

People often quote Matthew 25:21 when God says, "Well done, my good and faithful servant!" Although this

Scripture takes on new meaning for me, there is one that makes my heart swell even more.

> "I have brought You glory on earth by finishing the work You gave me to do." John 17:4

It's not only what I get to hear from God, but what I will someday be able to stand before Him and confidently say – that I finished the work He entrusted me to do. I'm not able to say that yet, but it will be my remaining life's mission to be able to.

In this moment, I'm thinking tenderly on the first chapter of this book. I was so scared and felt so unprepared for the pages that would follow.

But God.

Jesus remained by my side and held my hand the entire time. When I was done speaking, Freedom embraced me while Joy danced around us. Guilt and Shame had left the room, for there was no place for them anymore. It seemed Embarrassment was still lingering back stage, but Redemption reminded me to focus on who I was, not who I used to be, and Mercy brushed the tear from my cheek. Before I knew it, Embarrassment was gone too. There was only one who was missing. I looked around the room for Love, who had first held the curtain open for me, but could not find him. It was then Wisdom revealed to me – it was Love who had been holding my hand the whole time.

Gratitude told us it was time to get to work, so Trust helped me gather all the sins I had dug up. Our arms were very full. Together, we knelt down and laid them at the feet of Jesus, to use as He saw fit. Jesus smiled, and gave an approving nod.

> "You intended to harm me, but God intended it for good to accomplish what is now being done, the saving of many lives." Genesis 50:20

My story may be coming to an end, but it's really just the beginning. It can be the beginning of yours too. It's a beautiful day, and the Son is shining. Walk with me, won't you?

Tell Them

Jim & Caroline Klug

Thanks so much for allowing me to share my story with you, and I hope you'll continue to be a part of our journey. We can move forward together at:

        Instagram: @CarolineNKlug

        Facebook: @CarolineNKlug

        Twitter: @CarolineNKlug

Caroline Klug

Pip Klug

Want to be friends with Pip on Facebook?

www.facebook.com/Pip.Klug

Check out my Instagram page where you'll find a Fur Baby story highlight just for her!

@CarolineNKlug

Tell Them

Kyra Pingel

Show some support and follow this
beautiful singer / songwriter at:

Instagram: @KyraPingel
Facebook: @Kyra.Pingel

Caroline Klug

Stolen
By Caroline Klug

Stolen is more than a fiction thriller. It's a biblical allegory about redemption. Available on Amazon and Barnes & Noble.

Seventeen and on the streets, Star is a runaway headed down a dark path. It becomes even darker when she catches the eye of a serial killer who holds her captive in a remote prison in the woods. Failed escapes, physical torture, and mental anguish mark her days in isolation.

Alternating chapters weave her story around Sarah, a woman riddled with questions about her own past, who suspects the man she lives with may not be what he seems. As the stories unfold and connect, perhaps there's a twist that will make you want to go back and read it again.

This story brings to life the anguish of isolation and the choices that paved the way into their prisons. It also brings the gentle whisper of love and the audacious hope of freedom. Stolen is a thriller that will take the reader on a journey of pain and terror, as well as an unexpected journey of redemption.

The Waiting Room
By Caroline Klug

If you're in need of a miracle, interceding for a loved one, or believing in God to move a mountain, getting on your knees is the easy part. The hard part is waiting. Not seeing the answers we long for can leave us feeling depressed and even doubtful. We begin fixing our eyes on the world around us, rather than the One who made the world.

Whether it's been a day or a decade, don't lose hope. You serve a mighty God, capable of doing immeasurably more than you could ever ask or imagine (Ephesians 3:20). Join me as we dive into God's Word for insights and reassurance during your wait. He has a plan for your life, and His timing is always perfect.

Available on Amazon and Barnes & Noble.

Caroline Klug

Caroline Klug is an author of inspirational fiction, using thrillers and short story collections as a way to bring insights to people all over the world.

In addition to fiction, Caroline writes Christian Living books that teach, inspire, and encourage.

To see other books by this author visit:
www.CarolineKlug.com

Tell Them

www.ingramcontent.com/pod-product-compliance
Lightning Source LLC
Chambersburg PA
CBHW020400080526
44584CB00014B/1104